THE

PAUSE

PRINCIPLE

THE

PAUSE

PRINCIPLE

HOW TO KEEP YOUR COOL IN TOUGH SITUATIONS

CYNTHIA KANE

WILEY

Published by John Wiley & Sons, Inc., Hoboken, New Jersey.

Published simultaneously in Canada.

For general information on our other products and services or for technical support, please contact our Customer Care Department within the United States at (800) 762-2974, outside the United States at (317) 572-3993 or fax (317) 572-4002.

Wiley also publishes its books in a variety of electronic formats. Some content that appears in print may not be available in electronic formats. For more information about Wiley products, visit our web site at www.wiley.com.

Library of Congress Cataloging-in-Publication Data is Available:

ISBN 9781394283408 (Cloth)
ISBN 9781394283415 (ePub)
ISBN 9781394283422 (ePDF)

Cover Design: Paul McCarthy
SKY10091811_112224

This book is dedicated to you, the reader. May it help you find more moments of connection even when it's hard.

Contents

Acknowledgments   *ix*

Introduction   1

Part I   Learning to Pause   11

Chapter 1   Why Is It So Hard to Pause?   13

Chapter 2   The Pause Principle: SOFTEN   21

Part II   The Pause Practices   33

Chapter 3   Sensation   35

Chapter 4   Own Your Discomfort   45

Chapter 5   Focus on the Present Moment   55

Chapter 6   Take a Breath   67

Chapter 7   Eyes Toward Another   83

Chapter 8   Need to Say   101

Chapter 9   SOFTEN Meditation Practices   119

Chapter 10   The Pause Principle in Action   143

Final Thoughts   151

References   155

About the Author   161

Index   165

Acknowledgments

This is my favorite section to write because I love being able to take the time out of my day to sit here and thank the people who made this book happen. I can't help but smile when I think of how this all came to be and thank the universe for opening the doors so easily. The path is set—just walk forward. Well . . . here we are! Thank you.

I want to thank Troy Mott from Backstop Media for bringing Christina Rudloff into my life again. Because of Christina this book exists. One call that led to a proposal to a meeting to a yes, and here we are. Christina, you have been an anchor for me throughout this process. You have made me feel so at home with Wiley, and I am so grateful to you for seeing my work and believing in it and wanting to go all in with it. Your belief is what kept me going. Thank you.

Anne Marie O'Farrell is one of the most kind, honest, and generous souls I've met. While you weren't able to represent me with this book, you went above and beyond to make sure I found the right literary home—thank you.

To my agent Rita Rosenkranz. I know the way we found each other was a bit unconventional, though I'm so thrilled you said yes to me, to my work, and this book. Having someone in my corner this whole time to run things past has been invaluable to me, and I never once have felt alone in this process. Thank you for going through this with me and sharing your years of experience. I'm so appreciative of all that you do.

I'm so happy I was able to connect with Tess Woods. Thank you for helping to spread the word about this book and find the right outlets who may be interested in what I have to say. And to the powerhouse of Matt, Alana, Leah, Polly, Liz, and Fred, wow, you guys, we did it! Thank you for all the energy you put into this book and guiding me every step of the way. To Tom Dinse, thank you for digging into the chapters and giving me your editorial feedback, and to the design team at Wiley, thanks for the rounds we did together on the cover—I absolutely love it! Kevin Gillespie, thank you for the cycle of reactivity image; it's still one of my favorites that I use all the time in my work.

This book has come out of the years I've spent working with men and women on helping them change the way they communicate, to become more responsive instead of reactive. Daily I'm aware of the reciprocal relationship between me and those I work with. This work isn't easy, and it takes a lot of courage to first admit something needs to change and then seek out a way for it to happen. I am so grateful for all those who I've worked with over the years. Each person has left an indelible mark on my soul and has helped me to grow in so many ways.

Since I was five years old I knew I wanted to write books. It was a clear dream and goal that continues to this day. And while the road hasn't been easy or short, the two people who have been there since my days of writing poetry under my dresser late at night are my parents. For every moment you have been there, and I'm so appreciative of your never-ending love and support. For every twist and turn and fall, you've been there to help me up and keep me going, and for every smooth sail and opportunity you've been right there cheering me on. Thank you for all of it. I love you.

To my big sis, gosh, you're such a light to me. Thank you for listening to me and telling me like it is. I love our weirdness and our yearly trip and our stories and our history. I'm glad you're always a phone call away because my life wouldn't be complete without you.

The Segraves/Garcia/von Hass clan, thank you for bringing me into your family and always being so supportive of me and my work. When we're all together it brings me such joy. There's nothing better than sitting around a big table, with lots of food, good conversation, good people, and lots of laughter. Thank you.

To my ride or dies Ingrid Nilsen, Brandi Buechle, Ashley Baker, Tini Rhufus, Laura Ressler, Ilva Tare, Susan Soloman, Jeremy Levitt, Andrea Pungoti, Alex Miezlish, you guys are the gift that keeps on giving. Thank you for listening to me talk about my work, the book, helping me look at different versions of the cover, and giving me your thoughts and opinions. Each of you makes the world a better place to live in. Thank you. And thank you, Sam and Kim, for always making life more fun and for being awesome cheerleaders!

I've had so many teachers and mentors over the years. Some I know personally, and others I've just consumed their work over and over again. My work is a combination of everything I've learned along the way, so thank you to Susan Piver, Sara McLean, Thich Nhat Hanh, Tara Brach, Jack Kornfield, Marshall B. Rosenberg, Jon Kabat-Zin, Sharon Salzburg, Peter A. Levine, Beth Jacobs, Sakyong Mipham, Dzigar Kongtrul, Gail Chapman, Dr. Stephen Porges, Joseph Goldstein, Gil Fronsdale, Pema Chödrön, Angela Lauria, Avalon Starlight, Dale Carnegie, Jack Canfield.

And finally . . . my tribe. My kiddos, Holden and Ryah, who give me opportunities to practice my work, daily. Thank you for making it all so fun and playful and for letting me know when I need to press the pause button. And to my main squeeze, Bryan, you make it all possible all the time. Thank you. Simpatico forever and always.

THE
PAUSE
PRINCIPLE

Introduction

Through your actions as a leader, you attract a tribe that
WANTS to follow you.

—Seth Godin

Let me be the first to welcome you here to this book. I know you're busy, you've got calls to make, and emails to respond to, you have meetings and family obligations, you have a life to be lived. I know how hard it is these days to take the time to sit and read, even when we know a book has the power to change the way we see and interact with the world and those around us. Because of this, I promise not to take your time for granted.

So settle in, and start here, as this introduction provides the basic foundation you need to understand what this book is about, why it's different than other communication books out there, and what it's going to teach you. I promise, you won't find any fluff in these pages—it was written with you in mind.

What Is This Book About? And Why Is It Different Than the Rest?

There's a lot of difficult, awkward, and intense conversations that need to be had when you're a leader within a company that can be downright uncomfortable. I'm sure you can name a few you've had even within the last week or month. And what's hard is that you want to treat others as you also want to be treated: to be fair and disciplined and to show your appreciation for your teams. Knowing their trust means everything, you want to make sure you have their best interest in mind and that you're continuing to create security for them and making the best decisions to help them grow as well as the company itself. While that's your intention, in the heat of a conversation, it may all come out completely different.

While not everyone is caught on camera like Travis Kalanick at Uber digging into one of his drivers, more and more of those in leadership positions are being called out internally for how their reactions or outbursts are causing a breakdown within company culture and environment. When we're in the heat of the moment it's hard to find the language to make it the best possible outcome. Where we want to bring people together and create a sense of trust and connection, instead we create a disconnect and divide, and soon our organization feels like a dysfunctional family—with rivalry, trying to one-up one another, and slamming the door too easily on the way out. Research from the Society for Human Resource Management[1] reports that in the five-year period between 2014 and 2019, toxic workplace cultures have driven 20% of US employees out of their jobs—at a turnover cost greater than $223 billion, while *Forbes* reports that companies with strong cultures saw a fourfold increase in revenue growth.[2]

At the forefront of creating a thriving culture is the way those in leadership positions communicate, especially under pressure. And if you're noticing that it's more and more difficult to keep it together in stressful conversations, you're not alone. According to "The Learning Habits of Leaders and Managers"[3] report, 50% of managers cited difficult conversations as the biggest challenge they face in their roles, and according to research by the US firm Gartner, 67% of managers feel uncomfortable with face-to-face communication with employees. This discomfort may be a reason we're seeing more recorded videos being sent by those in charge either communicating layoffs, changes, or responding to challenging questions. There's even data that claims that 34% of managers admitted to putting off having difficult conversations for at least a month and that 25% had put it off for over a year.[4,5] Why are we so scared of these kinds of conversations? Not only because of the other person's reactions but also because of our own! The Chartered Management Institute (CMI) research cited that 43% of senior managers admit to losing their temper and shouting when placed in a difficult conversation, while 40% have admitted to panicking and telling a lie.[6] And it's miscommunications like these that cost companies with 100 employees an average of $420 000 per year.[7]

What's happening then? What's making it harder to be wise in the room and have calm conversations now more than before? The daily stressors and challenges of being a leader, that's what. There's having to work nonstop, needing to fix fires, pivot instantly, improve relationships between employees or within a team, moral and financial challenges, mistakes being made during crunch time, having to constantly adjust to demands, and let's not forget also having to answer to bosses, boards, shareholders, customers, numbers, what's happening in the world, and insert whatever else has your mind running laps here.

Being in charge means you're having multiple conversations in your head and with others at all times. And I'll say what we all already know, COVID has added a whole new complicated conversation to the already existing pressures, with people not wanting to come back into the office, negotiating remote and hybrid work, higher employee turnover, loss of company loyalty, and on it goes. We want to be that open, trusting, and appreciative leader in these tough situations, but the conversations we have to have today can make it hard to do.

Handling stressful conversations without blowing our top or getting passive-aggressive, defensive, dodging, or shutting down has always been good for business, but now more so than ever.

As mentioned, COVID has truly changed the landscape of work: where before people may have stayed within a team or company where the leadership was rude, dismissive, or aggressive, now employees are less likely to stay, and CEOs and managers are being asked to leave or are being pushed out.

Given that there are about 11 million meetings held every day and the world's challenges continue, it's safe to say that you're going to find yourself in many more difficult, awkward, stressful, and high-stakes conversations as time goes on. So who do you want to be in those moments? As someone in a leadership role, what you say and what you do matters. It is you who others are following, imitating, and influenced by; it is you who sets the tone. A Gallup study found that 70% of the variance in employee engagement is directly related to the manager.[8] Frontline managers, in particular, are the most crucial lever when it comes to engaging an organization's employees. That's a big responsibility to have as it means that the way you handle tough conversations has the potential to make or break the bottom line.

Most companies try to fix "heat of the moment" reactions by enlisting employees in communication courses or training on effective communication skills. Here the focus is usually on active listening, speaking, and breaking off using dialogue partners. These programs give instruction and information, and people will often leave with a script to use. Then what happens? The course, training, is over, the employee is dropped back into the real world, and everything they "learned" doesn't work—they're still being derisive and antagonistic in tough situations, and they're wondering why. Why did these theories work in a controlled environment but out in the wild I'm making things worse? Has this ever happened to you? It's definitely happened to me. Here's what the issue is—we don't see communication as a practice; we see it as a learning objective—and we are all focusing on the wrong part of communication.

Austrian psychiatrist Viktor Frankl wrote that "between stimulus and response there is a space. In that space is our power to choose our response. In our response lies our growth and our freedom."

To keep our cool in high-pressure moments, we need to put our attention not on the words we use or how we're listening but on that split second between the other person's words and our reaction—the space in between. How can we expand the space in between, lengthen the time between the stimulus and the response so we can choose calm, clarity, and compassion toward others in moments we maybe want to go for the jugular, overexplain, or run for the hills?

As you can see in Figure I.1, the text inside the large circle is what we usually focus on when it comes to communication—the automatic reaction or default reaction. This means we spend a lot of time trying to fix this part by learning how to say the right thing and listen in the correct way so as not to ruffle any feathers. However, changing our default reaction and saying the "right thing" and listening more skillfully isn't possible to do or maintain until we learn more about this little circle down at the bottom—the space in between.

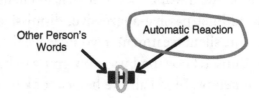

FIGURE I.1 Old focus of communication (big circle) vs. new focus of communication (little circle).

This little circle is the key to disrupting the speed at which heated moments begin to unravel. If we can master this moment and put our attention here, then we can handle whatever challenging conversation comes our way in a way that we respect and others admire.

What is this space in between? A pause.

You might be thinking, right, *Right, I've heard this before*, and it's because you likely have. It's easy advice that has been handed down from generation to generation, and it goes something like this, "All you have to do is pause before you speak." How many times have you heard it said? And usually within a bulleted list on someone's PowerPoint or as a subheading with a dedicated paragraph within a book or as advice from a friend or parent. The suggestion is a good one, though it's normally glossed over and not given much attention, because it sounds so simple to do. Well, here's the news-flash: it's not simple at all. If we all were able to pause in these hard conversations, then we wouldn't be seeing so many adult temper tantrums in the headlines. Pausing is not something we inherently know how to do or can do. It's also not something others teach us how to do, especially in heated conversations.

Until now.

This book is here to help you stay cool in tough situations by learning how to pause. A simple concept that is hard to implement without direction.

This book isn't based on theories; it's based on my own experience of learning how to show up differently in tough conversations. It took me a while to admit that in challenging conversations I would get passive-aggressive, dismissive, defensive, and give others the silent treatment. I would leave these moments feeling stressed, upset, knowing I was now going to have to repair the situation somehow. I read all the books, took tons of classes, went to retreats, had coaches, but it was one weekend seminar in New York when I had my aha moment. That weekend I was introduced to meditation and mindfulness, and what I figured out was how my reactivity began way before words ever left my mouth; my reactivity began in my body.

I started then playing around with mindfulness practices to regulate my body within a difficult and intense interaction to calm my reactivity. By doing this what I learned was how to carve out, extend, and make bigger that little circle from Figure I.1. I was learning how to pause and expand my capacity for discomfort in uncomfortable conversations so I could interact skillfully within them.

When I figured this out I felt as if I'd unlocked some kind of superpower—a place within that I didn't know existed and where I had more control of the chaos and uncertainty I felt in those interactions. Suddenly, I wasn't reacting defensively or passive-aggressively anymore—instead, I was choosing my words more intentionally, which was changing my relationships and repairing broken ones. I loved the freedom that came with this new practice, and I wanted to share it. For over a decade now, I've been working with CEOs, company presidents, HR professionals, financial planners, managers, educators, parents, caregivers, therapists, executives, nonprofits, and coaches—showing them how to create this pause within strenuous conversations, giving them in-the-moment practices to not get caught up in the cyclone that intense discussions can become.

I've had experiences in the past working with pretty volatile bosses, and all the time I wondered what I could do to change the situation, or better yet, how to avoid the reactive outbursts; if I just spoke in this way or maybe didn't go on too long, then the anger wouldn't erupt, and I wouldn't go in to questioning my sense of self and value added to the team and company. I put a lot of pressure on myself to make meetings and one-on-one interactions easy and relaxed, though when I look back now, yes, I did have a responsibility for how I was speaking and reacting, but so too did the one in the leadership role. For years I figured out how to manage my bosses' yelling, passive-aggression, and dismissiveness, and it shouldn't have been my responsibility to do so.

Most of the people I work with want to do better for their teams, clients, families, and partners, and they know that difficult conversations are essential conversations for growth. They want to speak with calm, clarity, compassion, and confidence, and they want to cultivate a space of trust and understanding in critical situations. It's a tall order and a high standard to have, though possible with the practices in this book. Maybe you picked up this book because you want to feel more confident within stressful conversations or you want to make sure you're being an intentional and responsive leader that keeps communication fluid and accessible with those around you. Perhaps you're looking for new ways to build trust and credibility. Or better yet, you want to create more engagement, dialogue, discussion, and to reignite meetings and talks where differing ideas bring about clarity and innovation. Whatever the reason is that brought you to this book, know that I'm glad you're here, and I'm excited to share this superpower with you—it's life changing.

What This Book Will Teach You

In Part I I'm going to cover what most people I work with want to know when they first come to this practice. I'll explain more about what's happening right now within tough conversations that make it impossible to pause. Then I'll share what's needed to be able to take that moment within stressful conversations and introduce the pause principle, which is to SOFTEN. You'll then get an overview of the pause practices, and then each chapter in Part II is dedicated to an individual practice.

The practices in this book are mindfulness practices that I've been teaching for over 10 years; they are concrete, tangible, and meant to be used in the moment, which means you'll be doing them within your conversations. Soon you'll know which ones work best for you, and they'll become your go-to pause practices for tough situations. You'll also be introduced to different meditations that will help you easily implement the pause practices you'll be learning, and then I'll hand over a five-day pause challenge and a 30-day pause plan for you to try out. And make sure to check out the links shared in the last chapter, where you can sign up to do the 30-day pause plan and get daily tips from me to help you implement the pause practices; there's also a link to get a free download of the pause principle workbook, which you can give to your team, do with your team, or try out by yourself.

What you'll learn here is how to self-regulate so that you can access yourself within the conversation and no longer be led and directed by the emotional overload. My hope is that these practices help you to stay in the room and actually have conversations, even when it's hard. And that when you're in a heated exchange, you'll remember the idea of softening and then intuitively grab one practice in that moment.

Years ago, I started sharing this work with others to help them pause in serious interactions, and every year since then, more and more people have benefited from the work. CEOs are finally talking, seeing more employee engagement and less turnover. Managers who weren't able to connect with their teams are being let in more and finding their groups are more productive and loyal. Educators are listening to one another after years of feeling unheard and unappreciated. It's possible to learn how to pause in a moment where you would usually lash out, shut down, walk away, get defensive, or overexplain; I do it, those I've worked with now do it, and so can you.

Pausing is an active mindfulness practice that you initiate within an interaction. And if you're anything like me, you'll be doing it multiple times a day for the rest of your life, in every area of your life. So if you're looking for theory and abstract concepts, this isn't the book for you. This is really a "get it done" kind of book, no fluffs and frills here, where even after a few chapters you'll be able to start pausing more. Like with anything new, it may feel strange or hard in the beginning, though I promise the more you implement these practices, the easier they become, and soon, they'll be like driving a car, riding a bike, or swimming in a pool—an embodied practice.

One important piece to note is that to be able to implement any of the practices in the book, you'll need to make sure you have read Chapter 3.

Ready? Let's do it.

Endnotes

1. SHRM. "SHRM Reports Toxic Workplace Cultures Cost Billions." SHRM Press Release. September 25, 2019. https://www.shrm.org/about/press-room/shrm-reports-toxic-workplace-cultures-cost-billions.
2. Laker, Benjamin. "Culture Is A Company's Single Most Powerful Advantage. Here's Why." Forbes. April 23, 2021. https://www.forbes.com/sites/benjaminlaker/2021/04/23/culture-is-a-companys-single-most-powerful-advantage-heres-why/?sh=487dac00679e.
3. Scott, Stefania. GoodPractice Insights: The Learning Habits of Leaders and Managers. GoodPractice. June, 2012. https://s3-eu-west-1.amazonaws.com/goodpractice-marketing/GoodPractice+Insights+June+2012.pdf.
4. Atana Team. "Why Managers Avoid Difficult Conversations," Atana. November 22, 2023. https://www.atana.com/blog/post/why-managers-avoid-difficult-conversations#:~:text=Among%20managers%20and%20workers%20who,off%20a%20year%20or%20longer
5. Bravely. "Understanding the conversation gap: Why employees aren't talking, and what we can do about it." Bravely. n.d. https://learn.workbravely.com/hubfs/Understanding-the-Conversation-Gap.pdf
6. Wilton, Petra. "The best strategies for difficult workplace conversations." CMI. July 29, 2015. www.managers.org.uk/knowledge-and-insights/article/the-best-strategies-for-difficult-workplace-conversations
7. SHRM. "The Cost of Poor Communications: The Business Rationale for Building this Critical Competency." SHRM. February 18, 2016. https://www.shrm.org/topics-tools/news/organizational-employee-development/cost-poor-communication#:~:text=Debra%20Hamilton%20asserted%2C%20in%20her,average%20of%20%24420%2C000%20per%20year
8. Pitonyak, Jon and Rob Desimone. "How to Engage Frontline Managers." Workplace. August 9, 2022. https://www.gallup.com/workplace/395210/engage-frontline-managers.aspx#:~:text=Gallup's%20most%20profound%20finding%20%2D%2D,to%20engaging%20an%20organization's%20employees.

I

Learning to Pause

Here we are.

At the beginning.

And what I'd like for you to do is fill in the stems of the following sentences. You can do that in your head or take a pen to the book—it's up to you.

If I paused 5% more in stressful conversations, I would . . .

If I paused 5% more in tough interactions, my working relationships would . . .

If I paused 5% more in high-stakes meetings, I would . . .

If I paused 5% more in difficult situations, work would . . .

You've now established that pausing would be helpful to do, so why is it so hard to do? This is what we'll look at first in Chapter 1 and then after you understand why it's not as easy as people make it out to be, we'll get into the pause principle in Chapter 2, which shows you how to make it easier, and then I'll give you the overview of the practices that are going to make pausing a reality.

1

Why Is It So Hard to Pause?

Man will only become better when you make him see what
he is like.

—Anton Chekhov

You've got this big idea. It's something you've been working
on for months. It took a while to move out of the details
and focus on the big picture, and you finally have the approach.
All that's left is to share the news and get your team to implement the vision. The moment you say it aloud, there's pushback. "We don't have enough bandwidth for this." That one
comment leads to a domino of reasons why this can't, shouldn't,
or won't happen in the way you dreamed or when you need it
by. Your anger and frustration come quickly, and within seconds
you're slamming your hand on the table, moving papers around
angrily and yelling. Maybe this behavior doesn't happen all the
time. Likely 95% of the time you can disagree and can hear

different voices and challenge them calmly, but this other 5% of the time, when you buckle under pressure, it feels impossible to not lose your cool. And what's hard is that these are the moments your team and those around you remember. What's most memorable is what's out of the ordinary—the moments that aren't routine. When the stakes are high and you lose your ability to respond in a measured and balanced manner, others see it, and when those in leadership roles breakdown, research shows, so do their teams.

It's been studied and decided that leaders who can't engage in dialogue under pressure create a negative impact on their team, leading to lower morale, lower quality standards, and missing deadlines and budgets (Maxfield and Hale 2018). Team members are more likely to leave their jobs, shut down, stop participating, and stop going above and beyond. While building trust and making your people feel safe can take years, losing integrity, credibility, and professionalism takes only a few seconds.

Conflict is a part of business (Douglass 2023), it's unavoidable, and most of us have been given the advice along the way to pause before saying something, and it sounds simple enough to do . . . but why is it so hard?

Why Is It Hard to Pause Under Pressure?

In the introduction I mentioned that most people and companies and organizations focus in communication training and workshops on how we speak and listen by providing scripts and using dialogue partners, etc. The reason a lot of the workshop content doesn't stick back in the real world is because our language and reactions are controlled by our biology, and, well, most communication courses miss the body completely. Communication is a body–mind practice, which means you can't pause in a high-stakes conversation without paying attention to the body first, thinking mind second.

When we start to look at our biology, we can see why it's so hard for us to pause in challenging conversations and also the way to make it easier.

Our Biology

Go back with me for a moment 200 000 years ago to the Stone Age. Here we are, living in a cave; our focus is on shelter, finding food, and protecting ourselves and those we love from predatory animals and the elements. There is not a moment where we aren't attuned to what is happening around us, so when a threat is known we're ready. If it's not the sounds that keep us up in our cave at night, it's the fear of infection, animals, or other tribes. We're always on high alert. To be on guard at all times we rely heavily on our sympathetic nervous system. The sympathetic nervous system is the fight, flight, freeze response (Taylor 2023). It is an involuntary physiological reaction that happens with a perceived threat. It starts in the oldest part of the brain, the reptilian brain (Baars and Gauge 2010), and releases tons of hormones—adrenaline, cortisol (the stress hormone), and these hormones then activate physical changes within us so that we're prepared to fight off a threat, flee to safety, or pretend we're dead so the big animal passes over us. These changes happen instantly, because they're designed to save our lives. Here's what's interesting: evolutionary psychologists have found that our bodies still react to a perceived harmful event, attack, or threat in the same way as it did back in the Stone Age. Today, we call this the stress response.

The Nervous System

There are two aspects of our nervous system: the somatic or the voluntary nervous system that controls all the voluntary muscles in the body such as moving our arms and legs. And then there's the autonomic nervous system, which is outside our control; this is food digestion, heartbeat, blood pressure. The autonomic nervous system has two branches: the sympathetic nervous system and the parasympathetic nervous system; both of these are always working within the body, and we shift between them during the day. The sympathetic nervous system is the fight-or-flight response. The parasympathetic nervous system is the rest-and-digest response. Understanding a bit about each of these is important, as we'll be working with both of them to be able to pause in heightened conversations.

The stress response is good when you're in emergency situations; however, any stressful situation (physical, environmental, psychological, or emotional) can trigger the stress response, and we know that the interactions we can get ourselves into at work are both psychologically and emotionally stressful. Instead of a lion that's threatening your survival, now it's conversations with your colleagues, employees, team members, administrators, shareholders, investors, even your partner and kids that are sending the nervous system into fight, flight, freeze. And this reactivity may be happening more often than before, because many of us are in a chronic state of stress day-in and day-out.

Right now, everything happens so quickly that it's hard to see the cycle of what's really going on in a stressful moment. Let's break it down.

1. You're in a conversation, and someone says something that pierces your heart—makes you feel unsafe, uncomfortable, in some way.

2. The amygdala turns on, which is the section of the brain responsible for fear. The amygdala then signals your hypothalamus, which stimulates the autonomic nervous system.

3. Your body senses danger or a threat and must protect itself. Your sympathetic nervous system kicks in and stimulates your adrenal glands to bring on the adrenaline and the cortisol. Your senses become sharper and more focused, you're more alert, your breath rate increases to oxygenate the body, your heart beats faster, blood pressure rises. Muscles start to tighten, and

4. You react instantaneously
   (a) Fight: You blame, yell, criticize, judge, stomp your feet, pound your fist on a table, slam a door, throw papers around the room, swear.
   (b) Flight: You walk out of the meeting; emotionally you have to escape because it's too overwhelming; you avoid, ignore, maybe seek out distraction.
   (c) Freeze: Your whole being is stuck, unable to speak, move, or make a decision. You're like an unplugged arcade game, completely shut down.

Take a look at Figure 1.1 for a visual of the cycle that's happening now.

Anytime we're in conflict or disagreement, where we feel attacked by someone's words, thoughts, ideas, or opinions, we perceive it to be threatening, and so the limbic system treats it as if it were a potential threat to our very survival. We react because this old part of the brain, the reptilian or primal part, takes over, making it hard to respond wisely and in a controlled and balanced way.

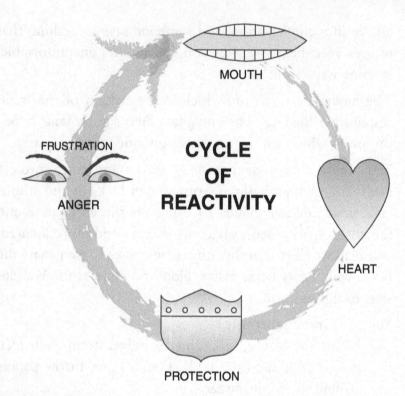

FIGURE 1.1 The cycle of reactivity: shows the cycle of what's happening now within our conversations that make them hard to pause.

Source: Kevin Gillespie.

Because we are wired to protect ourselves, reactive you is running the show, which is making it impossible to pause and lead intelligently in these conversations. It's a sweet gesture on our biology's part; however, in our working world, this isn't the kind of safeguarding we need. While it may feel like this is the only option available, it's not. We also have the parasympathetic nervous system.

Where the sympathetic nervous system is the flight-or-fight response, the parasympathetic nervous system is our "rest, digest, and relax" response. While you may not feel at ease in tough spots, you've definitely experienced the parasympathetic system before.

Maybe it's that early-morning moment where it's quiet and you and the birds are the only ones awake. Or when you're on a walk, after a workout, watching a sunset. It's that moment of exhale, where everything loosens, and your mind isn't directing the way. We're such a doing and thinking society that it's often hard to access these moments. I've worked with many leaders who find this place of rest to be uncomfortable, more stressful than the office, because it can feel as if they're not doing anything, as if they're being lazy, or it feels selfish and unfair. What they begin to see and learn is how crucial it is to find this place of rest in the body to be able to pause so they can be candid, curious, willing to listen, open minded, make informed decisions, and cultivate a healthy team and company culture; it's what differentiates great leaders from average or poor ones.

The parasympathetic system is activated when you feel safe and it allows the body to function optimally, creating an environment for tissue healing and restoration. Here the feel-good hormones increase and the cortisol and adrenaline decrease. The heart rate and blood pressure normalize, circulation improves, our immune system strengthens, our muscles relax, we can see the bigger picture. When we're in our parasympathetic nervous system we're able to problem solve, think clearly, be more intentional with our actions and words.

The move in the conversation from chaos (sympathetic) to calm (parasympathetic) is the pause itself; it is the moment between stimulus and response.

To pause is an active practice. Think of it like subbing in a sports game. You're intentionally stopping the play so you can take out what isn't working, and bring in what will. In the context of conversation we interrupt the sympathetic nervous system, take it out of the game, and sub in the parasympathetic nervous system. Check out the subbing in Figure 1.2 to see rest and digest sub in for the fight-or-flight response.

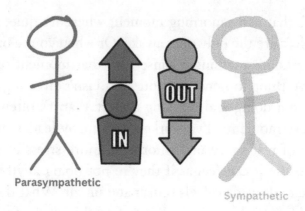

Parasympathetic

Sympathetic

FIGURE 1.2 Parasympathetic nervous system subs in for the sympathetic nervous system.

We want to be able to access our parasympathetic nervous system within difficult conversations. So essentially what we're learning to do is to take the sympathetic nervous system out of play and sub in the parasympathetic.

Now I don't want you to think the sympathetic nervous system is bad, because it's not. Or that the goal here is to get rid of it, because it's not. We need both of these systems to function properly and keep us protecting and enjoying our lives. It's more that for us to be more adaptable and compassionate and balance policy and politics in tough conversations with skill, we need to find a way to disrupt our stress response and switch into calm.

Now you know our biology (sympathetic nervous system) is what prevents us from pausing in stressful conversations and that to pause is the act of accessing more of our parasympathetic nervous system in these moments.

This all sounds great in theory, but how do we actually do it? Let's get into that in the next chapter.

2

The Pause Principle: SOFTEN

If our nervous system detects safety, then it's no longer defensive.

—Stephen W. Porges

We are wired to react quickly, so when there's a mistake with packaging, or someone isn't doing their job, or a team member questions the value of a project or has a different opinion on strategy, or maybe it's a clash over budgets or long overdue firing we pounce or are poised and ready to defend, attack, or shut down. We're in survival mode, and our fists are clenched creating more challenges than providing much upside. This way of reacting is easy to do, because it's natural for us; what's more difficult is to do the opposite. To feel calm in situations where we feel attacked. This act of pausing isn't something that just happens to us; it's something we make happen, something we intentionally choose to do.

In 1994, Dr. Stephen Porges proposed the polyvagal theory, which links our autonomic nervous system to social behavior. Remember that the autonomic nervous system is what's outside of our control and has two branches, the sympathetic and the parasympathetic systems. What he found was that when we experience feelings of safety, this keeps our autonomic nervous system out of states of defense. So if we can find a way to feel safe within difficult conversations, then we can move ourselves out of the stress response. The act of moving the body out of self-defense and into safety is the pause.

When we're in survival mode, we're like knights in armor. Covered head to toe, fighting and fending off those that challenge, question, or surprise us. With our swords drawn we protect ourselves, not wanting the other person to pierce our dress for fear they'll reach what lays behind. And while this armor is needed at times for protection, it is what keeps the battle going, saying over and over again it's not safe, you're not safe. What happens though when we take the armor off, hang it up for the day? Well, that's when we relax and soften the body, we kick our feet up, and our body feels safe, at rest. We know that to keep ourselves out of reactivity requires that we experience feelings of safety, so then how do we take this armor off while we're in heated interactions? We soften.

What Gandhi said is correct, "You can't shake hands with a clenched first." There's no chance of fostering community and an exchange of ideas if we're stiff. I used to practice aikido, I say that lightly, because I got as far as my yellow belt. But what I learned within it was how relaxed the body must be when someone is attacking. If I am tense and my body muscles tighten and harden, I'm done for, in that I'm easily pushed off balance or easily broken. If I loosen my body, and drop my weight, and soften, then I'm able to pause—make choices, guide, maneuver, and work with the other person. This is what we're after within heated conversations, the act of softening.

Scared to Lose Your Edge?

Those in leadership are often scared of losing their edge. They don't want to be too soft or too Zen, because they're nervous to be more human in a work setting. It's more professional to be at odds, cold, serious, standoffish, untouchable, inaccessible. Since being human isn't necessarily what got them to where they are in their careers to begin with, they aren't sure if the act of softening is for them. I would raise an eyebrow if some people didn't think this was a bit outside the box; however, at the end of the day what's most important is for the work to get done, the bottom line to be met, and everyone to go home feeling fulfilled and of service, and if that's the experience people want, then learning how to soften in the moments we want to be hard is the way to get it.

When you start softening, you start pausing, which gives you an opportunity to motivate and move forward instead of de-motivate others and stay stagnant. It's easy to give over to our instinctive behavior, it's much more difficult to find new and creative ways to nurture and be kind, honest, and helpful with a team.

I wish it were as easy as saying, now go on and relax within your conversations. But when has someone ever told you to relax or calm down and it actually happened? Likely never. What I'm going to do instead is introduce you to the softening practices, which you will try out and which will help you pause within hard conversations. Take one of the pause practices, implement it at the right time, and voilà . . . you're able to access yourself again under pressure and guide and instill pride and provide support. Figure 2.1 shows what this looks like.

FIGURE 2.1 The cycle of softening: This is the new pattern we're looking to implement so that we can keep our calm within stressful conversations. Instead of protecting ourselves, we use a SOFTEN practice to pause and then keep the integrity of the conversation intact.

This looks a bit different than the cycle of reactivity (Figure 1.1), right? No more shields and armor, no more automatic reactions that prevent dialogue and discussion. At the height of the pandemic most, if not all of my clients, were struggling with managing their teams. Conversations that they'd never had before, juggling of fears of those above them and those working with and below them, more responsibility of figuring out how to implement new policies and procedures for remote work, and handling pushback. Everything was on fire, especially their nervous system, and their shields were up. And on top of the stress inside their companies there was also the uncertainty of what was happening outside its doors. Learning pause practices is what helped my clients get through this storm intact. They were able to expand their capacity for discomfort, sit within the chaos inside and out, and guide these tough conversations without getting swept away by the size of the waves.

In this chapter I'm going to give you a high-level overview of the softening practices. I'll share what each practice is and how it helps us pause; then the chapters that follow are dedicated to each specific practice and how to do it, making it easy for you to reach for, find, and implement.

The Pause Principle: SOFTEN

When I first start working with clients their eyebrows raise when I share with them the pause principle, which is to SOFTEN. There's a lot of discomfort around the word itself. *Won't others walk all over me, take advantage or think I'm not fit for the position I'm in?* And what I say is this: Softening is what helps you connect with those you work with; it's what allows you to be heard and understood and human in the moments where your people need you to be. Softening is what gives you the opportunity to think clearly, live into the Albert Einstein quote of, "You cannot solve a problem with the same mind that created it." In heated moments, it's turning the body and mind from ice (hard and impenetrable) to water (soft and fluid).

What Are the SOFTEN Practices?

The SOFTEN practices are mindfulness-based practices. What this means is that to be able to implement them we have to start to bring an awareness to what we're doing in the moment we're doing it, what we're saying in the moment we're saying it, and what we're feeling in the moment we're feeling it. This attention to the moment we're in is a gentle and friendly attention—think light touch, not fixed or focused. The awareness of what's happening while it's happening is what we need to be able to sub out the fight-or-flight response for the "rest and digest" state.

What mindfulness helps us to do in our conversations is slow it all down and observe what's happening instead of being and becoming what's happening. When we start to be more of a bystander, watching and aware, we understand more clearly the cycle of reactivity, when it's happening, while it's happening, and are then able to implement SOFTEN practices to interrupt the pattern so we no longer react in the same old ways that are hurting not only the organizations we're a part of but also the trust in our leadership. Without awareness we'll fall into the same cycle over and over again.

To pause we need to be less consumed by what's happening in the conversation and instead be more mindful of our biology and the practices we can do to shift from feeling threatened within the conversation to feeling more secure and comfortable.

The SOFTEN Practices

My daughter loves to do art. Morning, noon, night, she's at the dining room table creating something. Maybe it's a rainbow factory or other days it's a unicorn family. Each time she draws she uses her Super Art Set. You open it up, and it's filled with crayons, markers, colored pencils, oil pastels, an eraser, scissors, tape, paper, and a ruler. She decides what she wants to draw, and then she chooses the right materials to do it. Think of the SOFTEN practices like your Super Pause Set. Here you're going to find different practices that work in challenging conversations. Just like my daughter chooses the best material for her projects, you will be picking the best pause practices that work for you.

The practices help you to regulate your body in the moment you want to shut down, yell, get passive-aggressive or run away. When you use these mindfulness practices to keep your calm during difficult interactions, you're having fewer bad days and more good ones.

Introducing the SOFTEN practices.

- S – sensation
- O – own your discomfort
- F – focus on the present

- T – take a breath
- E – eyes toward another
- N – need to say

Sensation

A client of mine was having trouble with someone else's team within her company. Basically, her staff was doing too much and taking on work that was this other team's responsibility, and the head of the other group wasn't stepping in to handle and take responsibility for the situation. When my client realized what was happening, she set up a meeting, hoping to find a solution. During their talk, the manager of the other team mentioned that the way things had been going seemed to be working. That one line sent lightning bolts through my client's body. It felt as if her insides were on fire. This is sensation.

There's a moment within a conversation where our body is signaling to us that we're not safe. I think of it like our body's own semaphore signaling system, think square red and yellow flags being waved internally in some kind of pattern. For the majority of those I work with, it's hard to feel any sensation of uneasiness or discomfort in the body during a conversation because their stress response is already on, but once they start practicing it becomes easier and easier.

The practice of noticing sensation in the body is a prerequisite for all the other pause practices, as it's the awareness of our discomfort in an interaction that signals it's time for us to use one of the other pause practices in the book. So make sure you read the next chapter before moving on to any of the others, because this is where becoming mindful of what's happening in the body during conversations is learned, and that's key to being able to pause.

When we don't listen to the sensation within our bodies, we act off instinct. We go directly into our reptilian brain, because our bodies feel threatened, so we're ready to fight, flee, or withdraw. There's no opportunity to pause, and rarely an effective conversation can be had under these circumstances.

Own Your Discomfort

My client with the lightning bolt sensation knew she was uncomfortable and in that moment she had two choices, ignore it or own it. Think of the times where you've experienced discomfort; what do you usually do with it? For me and those I work with, we like to ignore it, pretend it's not there, or get rid of it as fast as we can. I don't think I've ever met someone who likes feeling uncomfortable. The reason is because we perceive uneasiness in a conversation as dangerous, which means our nervous system is like, hey, we gotta protect ourselves now, and that's when we say things we don't mean and overreact. To be able to pause we practice instead owning the uneasy sensation, acknowledging it and soothing it, because when our discomfort is seen by us and calmed by us, it creates the bridge between stimulus and response.

Focus on the Present

Let's keep with my lightning bolt client. There she is, her insides catching fire at what the other department head has said to her, and she's so focused on getting his team to take back the extra work her team has been doing that she's becoming argumentative, and there's bits of passive-aggressive behavior being flung here and there. She is fixated on getting her and her team's needs met, though her reactive behavior isn't moving her toward her goal. The pause practice here is after noticing the uneasy sensation to focus on the present moment instead of the desired outcome.

In these moments we can get so caught up with what we're trying to do or the words of the other person that our nervous system is in overdrive. Refocusing and redirecting our attention to the present moment helps us find our way out of the never-ending cycle so we feel grounded, balanced, and centered again.

Take a Breath

I've been wanting to find a way to add cardio to my workout routine and so I joined Orange Theory. What I like about it is that you wear a heart monitor that is hooked up to machines so it tracks your heart rate during exercise. When you use a certain percentage of your heart different colors come up on the screen, so you know how hard you're working. The base level is green, and when you're pushing your heart more it's orange, and when it's all out it's red. The other day in class we were doing intervals where we would increase our speed to be in the orange zone for four minutes and then we'd lower the speed to find our base for a minute before another push for the orange zone. It's hard to get back to a base heart rate in one minute once it's been elevated, and the only way to do it is to know how to breathe. The moment when personalities clash our heart rate increases, we're not all the way into the orange zone like when we work out, but it's elevated. The pause comes in that moment of moving yourself out of the orange zone within a conversation and into the green zone, the journey from one to the other, and in this pause practice we do that by learning how to breathe in a moment when we feel we can't.

Eyes toward Another

What brought one of my clients to me was he was about to close a deal, and both sides were in agreement on all but one item in the draft. This sent him straight to the orange zone, and because he couldn't keep his emotions out of it, he was replaced. They had to find someone who could pause when challenged and who could talk to the other side to reach an agreement. We're very focused on our own agendas, and when we notice the sensation of discomfort in the body, because we aren't getting what we want, we can use the practice of turning toward the other and seeing them less like a lion and more like a human and then pause.

Need to Say

Before a town hall, presentation, meeting, or even an important phone call or conference you likely sit for some time mapping it out or have multiple rounds of conversations with others about how to approach it—what could happen, how to anticipate certain responses, what the purpose is, and the language by which to get there or the points to share. You edit out what's not necessary to focus on so it's clear and concise and easily digested. We plan for important conversations and meetings by focusing on the words we're going to use with others, and we rarely if ever think about what we need to say to ourselves to keep our cool during these moments. Since we're moving to body first, thinking mind second, we want to start to make sure we have language that helps our nervous system feel safe in these moments. This way we don't leave interactions surprised and frustrated that it went off the rails; *how could I have missed that, said that, been so insensitive, pushed too much, been so aggressive and contentious.*

These practices will make the stressful and challenging conversations easier to navigate; they will help you stay rational and be more in touch with those you're working with, showing yourself and others that you can handle the pressures that come with your position.

What to Remember

- These practices are mindfulness practices, which means they only work if you start to bring awareness to what's happening now within your interactions, without judgment and evaluation. You can't choose another path without being aware of the one you're on.

- The S (sensation) in SOFTEN is the prerequisite for the other five practices. You can think of it like S + OFTEN.

- You'll choose a few practices that resonate with you, try them out, see whether they work. The ones that work will become your go-to pause practices.

- These practices will help you be the leader you know you are and repair the one you've been.

You know the basics; now it's time to get into the details of how this all actually works and start putting it into practice. So . . . let's get it!

II

The Pause Practices

Right now, we're all walking around with different stories, past experiences, levels of education, thoughts, feelings, beliefs, and opinions, and yet what we all have in common is the ability to get upset, frustrated, irritated—to overreact, say things we don't mean, not say things we should say, shut down, dismiss, dodge, etc. We all do it—some of us more than others. And what is also interesting is that we are all walking around, different as we are, with the ability to pause as well; we just haven't been taught and don't know how to do it. What follows in this part of the book is the how.

CHAPTER

3

Sensation

In order to change, people need to become aware of their sensations and the way that their bodies interact with the world around them.

—Bessel A. van der Kolk

Oprah Winfrey said that "Leadership is about empathy. It is about having the ability to relate and to connect with people for the purpose of inspiring and empowering their lives." Of course this is what we want, and yet it's also hard to do, especially on the ground when negotiating, giving feedback, managing clashing personalities, sharing upcoming changes, answering to bosses, and trying to get what's still to be done before the end of a quarter. We know that how we relate in these tough moments matter, which is why learning how to pause is imperative. It gives us that empty beat within an interaction to make intelligent choices. As I mentioned before, the pause happens when we mindfully move our body from feeling threatened to feeling safe.

So before we can do any of the pause practices that come in the next chapters, we first have to know that we're in a heightened state to begin with, which is what this chapter will help you figure out. To know when we're uncomfortable we start to pay attention to our body sensations within tough conversations. In this chapter we'll dive into sensation and learn what it is, how to identify it, the three basic sensations within tough moments, and what your unique sensational reaction is.

Fun Fact

This knowing what you're feeling the moment you're feeling it is a sense called *interoception*. All the time it's working, monitoring the body, gathering data on how everything's feeling, and then your brain takes that information and processes it into a thought. Interoception awareness is extremely important for self regulation—emotion, cognition, and behavior.

What Is Sensation?

It's nonstop from the minute you walk into the office. There are emails to respond to, calls to make, people to meet with, and somewhere in there your stomach starts howling at you, it gurgles a bit, there's a tightness in the throat, you look at the clock and decide to pass off lunch and move on to the next thing on the to-do list. By the time you look up again it's the end of the workday, your breath smells like coffee, and you realize you haven't eaten anything besides a handful of M&Ms that you grabbed out of the candy bowl in the kitchen the entire day. This scenario has at some point happened to all of us. Our body tells us something, and we ignore it. From the minute you wake up your body is updating you on how it slept, how it feels, what it needs and wants. The way it communicates is through sensation. Sensation is immediate.

Take a look at some of the common sensations those I work with feel during tough conversations:

> tense, tingling, twisting, twitchy, throbbing, tightness, queasy, clenching, contracted, knotted, blocked, closed, burning, hot, breathless, buzzy, spacey, pounding, congested, heavy, pit in stomach, jumpy, jittery, jabbing, butterflies, full, pressure, pulsing, sizzling, numb, squirmy, trembling, stinging, wobbly, pounding, thick, fiery.

Have you ever felt any of these? Usually these sensations show up in the ears, nose, jaw, hands, feet, tongue, chest, stomach, and legs. Within conversations we either feel sensation and ignore it or we aren't aware of it at all.

Reflection Time

Take a moment and think about which sensation you are likely to have. Think back to the last difficult interaction you had . . . were you aware of sensation in your body and ignored it, or did you not feel it at all?

We don't usually pay attention to what's happening inside us during conversations, which is why we miss the cue we need to change course, pause, and not let the emotion take over and drive the dialogue . . . until now. Now you're going to be taking on the role of an observer of what's happening within you during stressful situations, you're going to gather information, not evaluate it, and the first thing you're going to pay attention to is which of the three basic sensations within hard conversations you're experiencing.

Three Basic Sensations in Tough Situations

Joanne is at the executive level within her company, and the talks and meetings about restructuring were now in play, which meant it was time to share the difficult information and let go of many people she'd worked with for years. She had a lot of questions about what to do if someone started to cry or if they got angry and yelled, possibly stood up and walked out and slammed the door without saying a word. Then she started wondering, *How do I not get emotional or upset during the conversation or what if I shut down and can't speak?* The answer: sensation. If Joanne could notice what was happening inside of her during the interaction, she would know how to pause the big emotions so she could be the compassionate and understanding leader she wanted to be in that moment. While each of us have our own unique sensations, which we'll explore next, sometimes it's easier to start with understanding the three general sensations we have within difficult situations. You might not always know what you're feeling or the specific sensation happening in the moment, but if you have a general idea of where it falls, you'll know whether a pause practice is needed or not.

Pleasant

Let's hang out with my client Steve for a minute. Steve had been at his same company for many years, and he was finally ready to move up in his career and start interviewing for more leadership roles within the company as well as look for other opportunities elsewhere. As you probably know, these days, there are multiple rounds of interviews that can last anywhere between 30 minutes to an hour. Interviews aren't easy; there's so much at play. It's a mix of not only Steve's experiences, how he responds to questions, will his personality clash or mesh with others but also how he does under pressure. If these aren't something that's being looked for in interviews, then there's a lot of quick turnover that's going to happen. To make sure Steve was the best version of himself, he started to pay attention in the first round of interviews to the sensation in his body. He knew from working together how important it was to keep his cool and pause where he'd usually like to go full steam ahead (he had a tendency to lose people as he would overexplain situations). During the first interview he noticed how calm, warm, relaxed, and comfortable he felt, how it all flowed. There was a sensation of openness and lightness. These sensations were pleasant. They felt so good that after the interview as he was preparing for the next one, that's what he wanted more of, these pleasant sensations.

Unpleasant

In his second interview he was introduced to new people within the company, and the questions became a bit more challenging. He noticed moments where he felt flushed, there was a pounding in his chest, and his throat was dry, which was making it hard to swallow. His stomach was doing somersaults, and when asked why a project failed under his direction he felt this fire start to well up inside. He knew all these sensations were unpleasant ones, and it's the unpleasant ones we have to be aware of. These were the ones that were about to lose him this opportunity, that could have him go from Mr. nice guy to Mr. defensive within seconds. He was able to pause and navigate the situation well; however, afterward he wasn't so sure that the position was for him. He wanted to do away with this uneasiness he felt as quickly as possible, forgetting that people in these kinds of positions are required to navigate discomfort skillfully.

Neutral (Neither Pleasant Nor Unpleasant)

By the time Steve got to the last interview he was beside himself. He still wanted the position, yet he wasn't as certain of it as he was after that first interview. While the second interview set him back a bit emotionally, he was confident in how he handled the pressure and was ready to show up as himself even more in this final interview. As he walked around the company and met more of those he would be working with he noticed an empty feeling inside. There was no sensation that was pleasant or unpleasant. It was like the back of the knee or the inside of the elbow . . . there, but not doing much. This sensation of neutrality can often feel like boredom in the body, that moment where you feel you need to get up and do something or you might lose it.

Because Steve knew to pay attention to his internal cues and understood the difference between pleasant, unpleasant, and neutral, he could move through the interview process without getting caught within the series of challenging questions and show how he could handle himself under pressure. As we start to pay more attention to what's happening within us, we are able to detach a bit more from the situation happening outside of us, which can help us not take things too personally.

Try It Out

Start to notice what basic sensation you're feeling within your conversations at work. There's no need to do anything about them; the idea in the beginning is to notice and become more and more familiar with when you're experiencing a pleasant, unpleasant, or neutral sensation. What this requires is that your attention moves from what's happening outside of you to what's happening within you. You're not spending a lot of time here—think of it like if you've heard a loud noise and you turn toward the sound to see what it is; then, once you've identified it, you go back to what you were doing before.

With these general sensations there is a tendency within situations to want to hold on too tightly to the pleasant feelings, fix and ignore or get rid of the unpleasant feelings, and be antsy and get up and do something with the neutral feelings. You can see how all of them can affect an interaction, and if the volume on any is turned up too loud, it could hurt established relationships. You can use the pause practices in this book after observing any of the general sensations you feel within an interaction, though the focus of this book is using them specifically after we notice an unpleasant sensation.

How to Identify the General Sensations in the Body

Because we're a thinking breed it can feel foreign to tap into and connect more in our body. How do we even know we're in our mind or in our body? If it seems hard for you, you're not alone. When I first started doing this work I didn't feel much in my body at all. Emotion, feeling, sensation gets pushed down over the years, and soon we can become more consumed with the mental chatter, it's the same for those I work with. Go ahead now and see whether you can put your attention on your head, move your attention to the forehead or the top or back, pick a place where thinking happens for you, and see what it feels like when your attention is on the thinking mind (all the thoughts going on in your head, the to-dos, the things you forgot to do, etc.). You can close your eyes if you want to. Now, go ahead and move your attention to the middle of your stomach, or wherever center feels in your body. You can even move your hand to the stomach as well. (If your mind starts talking again, notice whether your attention moves to your head; that's the mind talking, so then redirect your attention back to the body). You can stop the exercise. Did you notice a difference when your attention was on your thinking mind and when it was on the body? When our attention is on our thinking mind it can feel scattered, chaotic, fuzzy, tight. And what about when your attention was on the body? For some there's more of a grounded, relaxed, opening sensation. Toggling your attention between the head and the body and noting what you experience is a good exercise for learning what being in the body feels like.

See whether you can get yourself back to your body now. While you're here, can you identify any pleasant sensations in the body (think rest, ease, openness, flowing, light)? Then see whether you can move your attention to any unpleasant sensations in the body (tightness, throbbing, heavy, sore, clenching). Then move your attention to neutral in the body (places that you don't usually notice—your knee caps, behind the knees).

Taking a few minutes to sit and move our attention through all three sensations within the body primes us for understanding what's happening within a conversation and when we may need to implement one of the pause practices.

Your Unpleasant Sensational Reaction

Knowing the general sensations is enough to start implementing the pause practices in the book; however, it becomes much easier to SOFTEN when you know your own unpleasant sensational reaction (USR). Like I shared above, for this book we're focusing on the unpleasant sensation that comes in stressful situations, as it becomes your cue to use one of the pause practices.

Think back to at least three conversations you had where you lost your cool. Can you identify what was happening in your body before you reacted? What was the sensation? For me it feels like fire rising in my body or sometimes a balloon expanding within me, my chest tightens, and there's an aching sensation in my throat. This may take you a minute to think about.

Does your jaw clench, your mouth get dry, or is there tension in your forehead? There is no wrong answer to this question. If you look back at three conversations, you'll see that the sensation is usually the same or there's some variation of it.

Take a look at the following list, and see whether your unpleasant sensational reaction is here.

Achy, sore, tense, tight, shaky, throbbing, pounding, queasy, spacey, breathless, twitchy, nervy, burning, fiery, pit in the stomach, frozen, icy, blocked, heavy, closed, heart racing, palms sweating, throat dry, clenched jaw, knotted, hot, burning, jumpy, pressure, jabbing, butterflies, tingling, contracted, hot, buzzy, congested, jumpy, jittery, full, pulsing, sizzling, squirmy, trembling, stinging, wobbly, thick, urgency, static, frantic, quivery, disconnected, crampy.

When I asked my son the other day what was happening in his body during a big moment he said, "It's like my heart disappeared and an emoji took its place" . . . so, again, it's going to look different for all of us! And if it's still not coming to you from this list, not a problem; keep on paying attention to what's happening internally in the uncomfortable conversations, and soon you'll find it.

Whatever is happening in your body the moment before you react is what I want you to get really familiar with. To become familiar means you have to start entering your conversations differently, more slowly, intentionally and mindfully, being more aware of what's going on internally while at the same time engaging externally. Think of checking in with your body more throughout the day, starting to notice it more and how it's doing and feeling. Even just asking yourself, "What is my body feeling right now?" can get you more in tune with this idea of body first while in conversations. The moment you start to feel the uncomfortable sensation in the body is your cue to use one of the pause practices that we're about to get into in the next chapters.

What to Remember

Before you head into the next chapters, make sure you can answer the following questions.

- What are the three general sensations you can experience in a conversation? And what do they feel like in your body?

- What are some of your specific unpleasant sensational reactions (USRs)? So what is happening in your body before you go into your default reaction (yelling, shutting down, getting passive-aggressive, dismissive, dodging, ignoring, walking away, etc.)

- After you notice your USR in a difficult situation what are you going to start to do next?

CHAPTER

4

Own Your Discomfort

If your compassion does not include yourself, it is incomplete.
—Jack Kornfield

You now know your body is sending signals to you all the time, and within a challenging conversation you have your own unique sensations that come. Maybe you've identified that your chest tightens, you feel queasy, or maybe it feels as if your heart is about to burst out of the body. And if you haven't found the specific sensation, not to worry, because you're becoming more and more familiar with how to identify pleasant, unpleasant, and neutral sensations in the body. There's not one person I've worked with who has liked putting their attention on the unpleasant sensation, and you can count me into this bunch as well. I like being positive, not dwelling on things, moving past things quickly so I can get to the next item on the agenda, so when a not-so-great sensation comes I want to completely ignore it. While that's a common reaction to discomfort, it's also what

makes pausing impossible to do. When we ignore the unpleasant sensation, it grows and then marries another unpleasant sensation, and then they have babies, lots and lots of babies, and
pretty quickly these babies are crying, loudly, and we're pacing
around the table, shaking our heads, unable to control ourselves,
or maybe we grunt, put our heads into our hands, and give the
silent treatment, become insensitive, walk out. What happens
though when we own the discomfort in the moment is we slow
everything down and soften, we move out of the stress response
and back to calm ground . . . we pause.

In this chapter we're going to focus on the Own Your Discomfort pause practice. You'll learn what it is, why it works, and
how to start implementing it.

The Practice: Own Your Discomfort

Ever since I can remember I've had a hard time with criticism—
constructive or not. From when I was young and writing papers
in school to getting feedback once I started working, I wasn't
the type to see the recommendations as helpful. Instead what I
felt in these moments was stupid. Stupid for not knowing what
I didn't know. For days I would be upset and angry with myself,
beating myself up for not getting it right the first time. This
thinking that I was supposed to know everything caused a lot of
problems—as it affected how I saw myself and what I thought
about myself. I'll never forget during college being asked to stay
after a class so my teacher could talk about a paper I'd just turned
in, and while standing there, my insides were boiling, as he continued to tell me what may have been something helpful. When
his lips stopped moving, I didn't say anything, I stood frozen,
quiet, and squeaked out a thank-you and walked quickly out of
the room. During conflict or confrontation my biology likes to
protect me by shutting all systems down—I get tunnel vision,

my hearing starts to blur, and then I want to run. I've walked away from and ran out of many tough situations before. And there's a lot of these moments that haunt me. One of the reasons I started playing around with how to regulate myself within difficult moments was because I wanted to learn how to stay in the room. And as a leader this is important for you too. Town halls, shareholder meetings, team members bringing you their concerns, clients changing their minds, your team having different ideas than you, funding challenges, colleagues who aren't on board—all of these you want to stick around for and navigate calmly. One practice you can use to do this is owning your discomfort.

What Is Owning Your Discomfort?

As mammals we're very keen on what's known as co-regulation—social interaction that helps us regulate our physiology (Dana 2023, 2024). I see it so easily with my children. When one of them is having a meltdown, the moment I go over and wrap my arms around them, they quiet, relax, and soon their bodies are back online. In business we also crave this co-regulation in times of stress, but our colleagues and teams aren't coming in for hugs; instead, they're on the other side of a room or table, their eyes are looking everywhere but at us, their faces show no sign of affinity, and we're left alone in the moments where we need kind connection the most. Because we aren't able to get the acknowledgment and support we need from those in the room, we have to be able to give it to ourselves. We learn in the moment to offer ourselves what we usually want from others: friendliness.

Just like a baby learns to self-soothe by sucking its thumb or curling up into the fetal position, we now in these intense situations need to find ways to see our discomfort, own it, and calm it.

Why Does This Practice Work?

Imagine you're outside on a beautiful day, the sun is shining, there's a bit of wind blowing. You're reading. You go to turn the page, and a bee comes along and stings you. Do you yell at the bee, or do you get up and tend to yourself? I hope it's the latter because there's no sense yelling at the bee! For most of us when we get stung by something, we turn our attention to the stung spot, see whether it's red, swelling up, blistering; we tend to it first before anything else. We pause by caring for the discomfort we feel.

Owning our unease means we feel the unpleasant sensation in the body, and we acknowledge it. This acknowledgment of the state of our nervous system calms our nervous system and regulates our bodies. All our body wants in these moments is to be seen and heard, and so when we move our attention toward the sensation, without evaluating it, the sensation changes.

Try It Now

Take a minute and see whether you can identify an unpleasant sensation in the body. Maybe your muscles are sore, there's a throbbing sensation in the lower back, or it feels like a race car inside going round and round the track. See whether you can put your attention on this sensation. And instead of being upset at it, or wanting to fix it or change it, allow it to be there; bring a kind and friendly attention to it. Notice whether anything happens to the sensation itself. Most of the time the charge of the sensation will lessen, the texture of it will change, maybe it gets smaller.

When the sensation neutralizes, it does so quickly. If you've ever experienced the sensations of anxiety, a racing heart, swollen tongue, dry throat, formula one drivers on autopilot in your mind, it can be so intense that we try to fix it, get rid of it, ignore it, pretend it's not happening. When we push it away, it swings back in, like a swinging door; it's when we turn toward it, hold the door open for it, invite it in, even when it's scary to do, and nurture it, that's when the sensation often leaves. As quick as the discomfort can come, it can go. And when the sensation goes, so does the feeling state along with it—anger, fear, anxiety, frustration, stupidity, etc.

Sensation and emotions go hand in hand, meaning there's a sensation to anger, anxiety, stupidity, confusion, feeling misunderstood, just as there is to joy, happiness, excitement, inspiration, etc. And if you want to and are in touch with your emotions, you can see whether you know what sensations match with what emotions; for everyone it will feel different. With this specific pause practice, what's most important is knowing that you're experiencing an uncomfortable feeling as opposed to the exact feeling that it is (the exact feeling is more important when we're focused on expressing ourselves, which we're not in this book). Think then whether someone you love is angry, scared, frustrated, or feeling stupid, their bodies are filled with sensation, which means their nervous system is in a heightened state, dysregulated, and in these moments you would likely check in on them to see whether they were okay or they needed help. This is now what you're going to be doing for yourself in these tough situations, checking in, supporting, and calming yourself.

What is hard about this is that our natural reaction is to protect ourselves in stressful situations, and that usually looks like the opposite of soothing ourselves. We harden and make solid, so when a task isn't turned in on time and a client is left hanging, we snap, jab, break down, or stand frozen letting it slide. A way to stop this pattern is to interrupt it with the pause practice of owning your discomfort.

Ready to try it out? Let's do it.

Sensation + Own Your Discomfort = Pause

When I first started working with Adriana she was having issues with an employee. Basically, they didn't get along due to their different personalities. Each time the employee walked into her office it ended badly. And Adriana was becoming known for being hyper-critical and having unpredictable behavior more than anything else. She wanted a way to pause before things went further downhill. We worked on first identifying the sensation in her body during these hard interactions. Her sensation was a tightness in the chest. Then it was helping her to own the discomfort by finding the right type of contact or touch that would calm the sensation.

We talked a few chapters ago about the nervous system and how the pause comes when we move ourselves from flight, fight, freeze to rest and digest; well, a way to get there is by activating the main nerve of our parasympathetic nervous system, the vagus nerve. This nerve is super long and runs from the brainstem to the colon; it's responsible for our heart rate, digestion, breathing, sneezing, swallowing, vomiting, sweating, speech; and it links the gut and the brain. When the vagus nerve is working properly, we're in a relaxed state, and all systems are aligned and working, but during emotional stress the vagus nerve can be triggered, sending us into our sympathetic nervous system (fight, flight, freeze)—creating the unpleasant sensations we're now familiar with and that Adriana identified for herself. To calm the body during stressful situations we want to find ways to activate the vagus nerve, and one of the ways is through touch.

Here are practices you can use in stressful interactions to help you pause and stay wise in the room.

Rub Behind Your Ears

When I hear this I automatically think about dogs and how much they love to have their ears rubbed. I'll go ahead and say that we aren't any different. Dogs have a vagus nerve as well and it runs from the base of their brain (around the ears) all the way down through the spine, chest, and into the abdomen—same as us. When you start to notice the unpleasant sensation in your body, you can easily bring your hand to your ear and start to rub—going behind the ear and also inside along the ear canal in a circular motion. While you're doing this, you're breathing long and slow breaths.

Pull Down on Your Ears

When I was in elementary school I had a Spanish teacher from Argentina. What I loved most about Spanish class was when we celebrated my birthday. Though I'm a June baby, Señora Astie would remember to celebrate mine before the end of school. On birthdays, she would stand behind me and gently pull on my ears; then when she got to the number I was turning, she'd tug on them. Little did I know that the reason I felt so safe and calm in that moment was because she was activating my vagus nerve! This is also something you can do while you're in a meeting or tense conversation—you feel the unpleasant sensation in the body, and then you gently rub down on an ear; it doesn't matter which one you choose. A reminder that we aren't doing these things in an exaggerated manner or to a point where it's distracting—this is only when we feel the unpleasant sensation in our bodies.

Rest Your Hand, Tap or Draw Hand Circles on Your Sternum

This is the practice Adriana chose. Right where a necklace would lay she started to rub in a circular motion, three times, and then let her hand rest there for a moment. This practice didn't change how she felt about the employee, though it did help her pause to be able to interact more skillfully. Rubbing or tapping the sternum has the same effect. What's interesting about circles on the sternum is that in sign language the word for sorry or apologize or regret is rotating a closed hand counterclockwise on the chest. In these tough situations where we crave co-regulation, what we're doing here is saying to ourselves, sorry that you're feeling so unpleasant right now—it's okay, we've got this.

Massage Your Jaw Line

One easy way to own the discomfort is by cupping your hand around the jaw and using your fingers to gently massage the jaw line. You may notice you do this instinctively, and it's your body reaching for something to help it feel grounded. And for those who have a beard, you may notice that even scratching the beard at the temporomandibular joint, where the lower jaw connects to the skull, or the motion of following the bone down the jaw line moves the body into a more relaxed state.

Massage the Side of the Neck (Back or Front)

Gently rubbing either the right or left side of the back of the neck is a great way to activate the vagus nerve. You can massage the front of the neck as well, the throat. It's not pressing down, but using circular motions on either side of the throat, with your index and middle fingers; you can also just do one side and then the other. Remember that it's gentle, no pressure.

Even if we aren't specifically activating the vagus nerve, touch is important to relaxing the body in stressful situations (Reynolds 2022). Touch helps us to reduce stress, lower our heart rate, and boosts our energy.

Next are some other practices you can try.

Havening Touch Techniques

- Take your right hand and place it at the top of your left shoulder and follow it down to the elbow. Silently say to yourself: "Be calm, relax."

- Take your left hand and place it at the top of your right shoulder and follow it down to the elbow.

- You can rub your hands over one another like you would while washing them under water.

- You can gently stroke your face as well while acknowledging your discomfort.

Finger Taps

To soothe ourselves within a conversation, we can tap each finger to our thumb, and while doing so, silently recite words, mantras, phrases. Some of my favorites are the Hawaiian chant, Ho'oponopono. The meaning of the name is to bring back into balance, and what I do is use the phrases while tapping. So, it goes:

Thank you, I love you, I forgive you, I'm sorry

In the moment of discomfort, we're offering to ourselves support, saying thank you for all you do, I care for you, and then forgiving ourselves for being upset or to our breaking point, and then apologizing to ourselves for it. Some others that have worked for my clients are:

- calm . . . begins . . . with . . . me
- pausing . . . begins . . . with . . . me
- everything is Okay
- you / we are Okay
- challenges . . . happen . . . in . . . business
- my . . . body . . . is . . . relaxing

And if using different words feels too complicated, you can either think of how you want to show up and be in these types of situations and use that word—kind, kind, kind, kind or helpful, helpful, helpful, helpful, or you can do away with the words altogether and just tap the fingers together.

Massage Pressure Points

There's a pressure point in the webbing or meaty part of the back of the hand, between the base of the thumb and the index finger, called the Hegu (her-goo) pressure point (Barkley 2024). When you feel an unpleasant sensation in the body and know that your nervous system is in a sympathetic state, you can apply pressure to this area, massaging it for about five seconds. This pressure point is known to release stress as well as headaches, toothaches, and pain in the upper body (neck and head). This is an easy practice to do every so often throughout a meeting, even before an unpleasant sensation occurs. If you're pregnant, you'll want to avoid this one, because it's known to induce labor.

Another pressure point you can try is called the Inner Frontier Gate Point. This one is on the inside of your arm. Turn your arm so your palm faces up, and then with the other hand put three fingers behind the wrist, find the hollow in the arm, and massage for four to five seconds. This pressure point is helpful to relieve anxiety and nausea.

Owning our discomfort can help us move our nervous system back into a place of calm, clarity, connection, so it is ready to handle the obstacle in front of us. These practices disrupt the automatic panic, fear, and frustration, and instead cue the body back to comfort and stability.

Make a Commitment

What are three practices that stand out to you? Or what three practices do you think would be the easiest to implement?

Write them down now.

1. _____

2. _____

3. _____

Choose one practice to try

_____

CHAPTER

5

Focus on the Present Moment

> Be fully present. Feel your heart. And engage the next moment
> without an agenda.
>
> —Pema Chödrön

I had a client, Leena, who would wake up before her family
and go outside for a walk or a run. She'd tell me how quiet
it was in the morning, how nice it was to be able to hear the
birds, watch the sun come up; she was filled with possibility and
excitement for the day ahead. For her the mornings felt as if
they existed almost in another realm, separate from the day and
disconnected from the night. As if she found the moment for
herself where time stood still, she could see easily, think clearly,
there was no fear, worry, stress, anxiety—no little feet running
around. Then as the day continued this mindfulness and present
moment awareness would vanish. Just like that, she opens the

door to her house, and it's time to get herself and young kids
ready for the day, off to school, and then she's on to work. She's
a new partner in a law firm and has recently been losing her cool
in meetings because of the pressure she feels to bring in new
clients with big budgets. It's not happened once but a few times
now, and it's started to affect how other partners engage with
her. When I talked with Leena I reminded her of her morning moments, where there was a sense of suspension, a place of
ease, presence, and connection, because this is the place we want
to cultivate within heated conversations. Finding the present
moment within difficult situations helps us move back into the
parasympathetic nervous system where all systems are function-
ing and we're feeling safe enough to continue a conversation,
especially when people disagree.

This chapter is dedicated to pause practices that help us focus
on the present moment, the now, in tough conversations.

The Practice: Focus on the Present Moment

Irene was a new hire on Luis's team, and it was during their
first meeting that Luis told her he didn't think her idea for an
alternative funding stream would work. At the next team meeting, she brought it up again, and again, he said he felt it was too
much of a risk. A week later she walked into his office ready to
state her case once again. At this point, Luis was so bothered by
what he felt was a lack of respect that his nervous system was
quick to kick in to survival mode. He felt the fire in his face, and
he knew he was about to get caught in what I like to call a conversation bonzo gonzo. For those wrestling fans out there you'll
know what this is, but for those who aren't, it's a term used when
all the wrestlers are in the ring and the referees can't get anyone
to rein it in. Luis had been in these bonzo gonzos before, and

on some exit surveys people had brought up how he can be rude with people and also overly sensitive, where his reaction doesn't match the issue at hand. This time, even though he didn't like Irene and it was a personality clash, he really wanted it to be different, as the company culture was something they were working on to prevent the uptick they'd seen in people leaving. He noticed the cue (the unpleasant sensation) and focused on the present moment, which took him out of the match completely. No longer armed and ready to go, he was calm, no longer feeling threatened.

I imagine this big arena; it's just him and Irene. Irene is standing in the ring, her arms up to protect herself, and there's Luis, relaxed enough now that he finds a seat in the stands. This is what focusing on the present moment does in a conversation: it transports you from inside the chaos to outside of it.

If we stick with sports for a minute here, think about all the coaches and where they are during a game, there on the sidelines, watching what's going on, thinking up the different plays, strategies, knowing what's working, what's not, seeing whose legs are getting tired and need a break. They are positioned to the side so they can make the calls, see clearly; they're not being moved around by the other players or the plays themselves—they're the ones directing the plays. The pause comes when you walk from the ring, field, court, rink, green, and the list goes on, to the sidelines because from here you can be the mentor and support you want to be.

Why Does This Practice Work?

Calvin is in real estate, and during the down market he had to negotiate with his client to reduce the price on his property. Not easy conversations to have when his client is attached to the number and Calvin is attached to the sale. When we're around a table, or in the ring, trying to make things happen, we're all attached to what our goal is.

- We want to get more money for our team—attached.
- We want to hire a new position—attached.
- We think the other person's opinion is mindless—attached.
- We want the deal to go through—attached.
- We want the trustee to call us back—attached.
- We want to be respected—attached.

When we're in the business of business it's hard to veer from a one-pointed focus. Within difficult conversations we're so attached to the outcome that it's easy to feel fear and panic if it looks like we're not going to get it. That fear and panic sets off our reptilian reactions, and we can no longer manage stressful conversations successfully. If, though, we detach from our desired outcome and instead focus on the present moment, then we can regulate our nervous system and access our prefrontal cortex, which is our logic and reason, and soon we're back to feeling calm, connected, social, and able to problem solve and emotionally regulate. By focusing on the present moment we remove ourselves from the heat and pressure and give ourselves the opportunity to cool down, get clear, and proceed. There had been times before where Calvin had lost clients due to these kinds of situations, as he would become inconsiderate or condescending during meetings. When he started to implement the practices in this chapter, he had so much more space and time to choose his words in tricky situations more mindfully.

Calm exists only in the present moment, and when we're in stressful conversations, we're taken out of the moment we're in and drawn into the issue or the challenge that usually pertains to the past or the future or a present moment challenge that affects the future or was created from the past. Focusing on the present moment in stressful conversations means we're actively creating presence (Petranker 2014), we're being actively present, which means we get to create calm and space so we can then choose how we act and show up as a leader.

Sensation + Focus on the Present Moment = Pause

When we use any of the pause practices in this book it means we're teetering on the edge of overreaction, we're aware of the unpleasant sensation in the body, and so we know: let's do something different here, let's interrupt this pattern. What this chapter's practice is all about is bringing our attention back onto the present moment, refocusing our attention. Think of it like if you're on the phone and then you start hearing your computer dinging with new messages coming in; each time that ding happens you have to mentally refocus your attention back to the person you're talking to, because all you want to do, like anyone of us, is move your mouse to activate the screen to look at the emails. It's extremely easy to lose the present moment within a heated discussion, and that's what we want to get back so that we can pause and emotionally regulate.

Take a look through the following practices. Not all of them will resonate with you, and that's okay. You only need a few to try and see whether they do the trick. And then once you've found what works, they'll become your go-to, in-the-moment, pause practices.

Ready to find the present in high-pressure situations? Let's do it.

Feet, Hands, Belly

When I ask clients to describe what it feels like within disagreements they often say floaty or scattered. It's like those inflatable tube men or air dancers you'll see outside car washes or other stores. One minute they're up; another minute they're down. One minute there over to the right, and then they're to the left. For me it sometimes feels as if I'm holding hundreds of balloons and I can't keep them all together. What we're missing within these conversations is a sense of feeling grounded and centered. We get caught so easily in the other person's language that soon we're all tangled up, trying to find our way out.

A great way to feel grounded within the conversation is to notice what your feet, hands, and belly are doing. Quietly moving your attention to your feet: *What are my feet doing?* Quietly moving your attention to your hands: *What are my hands doing?* Quietly moving your attention to your belly: *What's my belly doing?* You're paying attention to the sensation in the feet, hands, belly, noticing them, seeing whether there's tension, and can you intentionally soften them. Seeing whether you can let the belly go if it's tense and start breathing into a soft belly instead of a hard belly. Some clients when bringing their attention to their feet imagine roots connecting them to the ground to help them soften and reset.

We aren't looking for that hard attention, that laser focus, but more a gentle, friendly touch of attention. You can play around with it now by moving your attention while you're reading to your fingers, to your shoulders, to your nose, and then to your belly. Now come back to the book.

What you'll begin to notice with these practices is that you have what's going on in the foreground, which is the conversation itself, you with others in a group, what's actively happening in front of you, and then you have what's going on in the background, which is what's happening with you internally. What we're doing is pausing the intensity of attention on the foreground and refocusing it on the background because what's happening in the background is what affects the foreground. If I find rest in the body and can soften my body, then my mind can relax as well. And once the mind is relaxed, the words are relaxed. These words then continue to create a culture and environment that people want to show up in.

Your Breath

We're going to focus more on breath in the next chapter and really get into different techniques; however, it's important to mention it here as well because it is one of the easiest ways to find the present moment within an interaction. Leading is hard, and when you're a part of a family business it can be even more complicated because you're dealing with relationships you've had since you were a tiny tot. There's a lot of stored memories informing your interactions. Anytime one of my clients met with her brother it always turned into something, so much that those in the office knew to stay clear of the meeting rooms and prepare for the aftermath. It wasn't a good situation as it had not only stalled out certain projects and also lost others, but it was also affecting those that worked there. We played around with finding a way to pause by accessing the present moment through her breath. When tensions started to rise, she would move her attention to the breath—the inhale and the exhale—saying to herself, *I am breathing in; I am breathing out*, and this helped soften the body so she could look at her brother and what they were working on together through a different lens.

Sense It Out

Right now, it's raining. If I notice the sound of the rain on my roof or the drops hitting the ground, I'm present. If while I'm writing I get curious about my fingers on the keyboard and what each letter feels like when I press down, I'm present, or when I can smell the coffee brewing on the stove and then taste it instead of drink it, I'm present. And when I choose to watch my kids come down the stairs in the morning, without evaluating or rushing them, I'm present. Right now, look around where you are, notice what you can hear, observe what you're touching, see whether there's a scent you're picking up, or a taste in your mouth.

Terry had been hired as a new manager, and she was wanting to make some changes within her department. She wanted to get the team to align with her decisions on funding goals, though during the meetings it was clear the team saw things differently. They voiced their opinions, saying this isn't how things have been done previously within the company. Feeling threatened, Terry lashed out, put her foot down, and decided to go with her decision anyhow. From this point on, the team was disengaged and on surveys shared that it felt more like a top-down approach than a collaborative one. We had started working together during this time, and so in the next meeting she was confronted with a different idea than hers, and she noticed the buzzing in her body and the clenched jaw, and then she saw her cup of tea. She paid attention to moving toward the cup and how it felt to reach for it. She noticed the weight of the mug as she picked it up. She inhaled the scent and then exhaled while she took a sip and tasted the tea. Those few seconds of pause helped her to soften and bring her back to the direct experience instead of getting caught in the match point of the game.

I tell my clients to SIP during conversations, which means to slow down, go inward, and get present. The more you can SIP, the more you can pause, and the easier the interaction becomes. Here are some ways to SIP.

- If you're out for a coffee, work lunch, or dinner meeting, you can use your food, beverage, and utensils and cups to bring you into the present moment. You can also rearrange your napkin to help you pause or clasp it between your hands to feel the fabric.

- In the office you can notice the texture of the paper in front of you, the pen you're holding, the sound of moving in the chair, the sound other people are making, rubbing your hands together noticing skin on skin and the heat it creates, or tapping your fingertips against one another observing the vibration that happens from it.

- Find something in the office that reminds you to notice the present moment. For some it's a decorative item in the room, or a picture on your desk; for others it's a plant or your pen holder; some use jewelry (rings, bracelets, necklaces), lamps, diffusers, even certain furniture can become a cue or a color. It's also not only for your space but also the environments you walk into. When you get there, see whether you can find something that immediately calms you by looking, touching, smelling, or tasting—then that becomes your go-to when you feel the discomfort in the body.

Hold Something

When we're in states of stress we're like a boat drifting out to sea; we're moved by it all, and every little wave feels like a big one; when we're in our stress response it's extremely hard to tell the difference between what's a little deal and what's a big deal. What can help is to create a sense of being anchored. A lot of my clients use this practice, especially those with ADHD, as it really helps regulate our nervous system in difficult situations. It's having something in our hands. It can be a stress ball, an old-school kush ball, a pen, a marble, a little figurine, a penny in your pocket, a small rock. A friend of mine even used Play-Doh once while on a difficult phone call, which she said helped her tremendously.

What's important is not only how it feels in your hands but also the weight of it—there should be weight to it: not too heavy but just enough to give the sensation of being grounded.

Thumb-to-Pinky Taps

The thumb is known in ancient Indian astrology to symbolize the personality. Because of this, in difficult moments, I like to hide my thumbs underneath my other fingers, as it cues me to relax my ego that wants to go full speed ahead. And the pinky is known as intuition, communication, and articulation. When we tap the pinky and thumb together, we activate neurons in the brain to help us slow down, focus, tune out distractions, be present, and choose our words carefully.

Posture

There's no class on it in business school, I don't think, though almost all leaders have gotten the memo that how they carry themselves is important. It's quite rare to walk into a room full of people and not be able to pick out, simply by how they're holding themselves, those who run teams. The good news is that studies have shown that the upright posture that you naturally carry, with your shoulders back and head high, is also doing wonders for your nervous system (South Loop Chiropractor n.d., Family Chiropractic Chatswood n.d.). Remember the vagus nerve we talked about in Chapter 4? This is the longest parasympathetic nerve in the body, and when it's activated we're clear and calm, and when it's deactivated we're in our fight, flight, freeze response. When we're hunched over and our head moves forward, the vagus nerve no longer works effectively, and we put ourselves into the stress response. This is all important because when we're in intense situations we can find the pause by shifting our posture, making sure we're still open and connected (Veenstra 2016; O'Toole and Michalak 2024; Carney, Cuddy, and Yap 2010). A study from Harvard showed that when people adopted more open postures and a straight spine they showed a decrease in cortisol levels (the stress hormone) (Cuddy, Wilmuth, and Carney 2012; Loncar 2021). Maybe this looks like standing up and walking behind a chair for a minute, rolling our shoulders back, moving forward in our seat to put our legs at a 90° angle, tucking the chin slightly to feel the stretch in the back of the neck.

Internally Broadcast What You're Seeing

When we're feeling flooded with sensation and we're on the edge of spiraling, even noticing and internally broadcasting to yourself what you're doing brings you back to the present moment. We all have heard sportscasters on television giving us the play-by-play of what's happening at the moment. This, then, is what you become in these tense moments, so it looks like telling yourself internally, *I'm sitting here right now. The cup is on the table. This person is talking to me. I can feel my feet on the ground. I am breathing in. I am breathing out. I can feel the air conditioner on my arms.*

Redirecting our attention back to the present moment helps us stay connected with ourselves during serious conversations and situations. Think of the leaders you admire, those who maybe when you were younger you looked up to and who mentored you, those who you've recently met or read about. They gave you something to aspire to—now that's your role for others. There was a clip I saw from the 86th Oscars of Matthew McConaughey's acceptance speech. And in it he talks about the three things he needs to be successful and do good work. He says the first is something to look up to, the second is something to look forward to, and the third is someone to chase. It's the third that I find the most interesting because he talked about how the person he's chasing is always his future self, 10 years from now. Our future is directly related to the present moment, as it's the present moments that make up our future. Each conversation you have, each tough situation you navigate brings you closer to the version of you and your life you're chasing. Accessing these present moments gives you the pause you need to tap back into yourself and choose the next moment skillfully; that is, does it bring you closer to or further away from your future vision?

Make a Commitment

What are three practices that stand out to you? Or what three practices do you think would be the easiest to implement?

Write them down now.

1. _____

2. _____

3. _____

Choose one practice to try.

_____

6

Take a Breath

Physical and emotional states can be altered by changing the breathing pattern.

—Wilhem Reich

When I was younger, camp was a big part of my life. Those two to three months during summer felt as if they lasted forever at that young age, and it's really where I found and discovered these two sides of me that to this day I work to balance. On one side of it all, I went to a camp in Algonquin Park in Canada called Tanamakoon. We slept in cabins, no running water, bathed in the lake with salt cans for the leeches, went on canoe trips and backpacking trips, did solo sits where they dropped me for an hour somewhere with only whatever vegetation was around me, and they were making solar cookies before solar even a thing. This environment and lifestyle made such an impact on me because it was the first time I felt I had time to breathe or space to be, where I felt relaxed. And I loved this space and freedom I found there. Loved it so much I went back years later to become a counselor in training. This was one side of me, and then the other went to Culver Military Academy for three summers. When I tell people this they often wonder what I did to be sent there, and while I did throw some raging parties growing up, it was more that my mom's brothers had gone there, my sister went for a year, and now it was my turn. What I found out was that there was this other side of me that absolutely loved and thrived on routine. I loved having a packed schedule and something to do all the time. I liked the team aspect of it all and working together and leaning how to compete, win, and be graceful. Sure, there were the things I didn't like, the checks to make sure our closets were organized and our clothes were put away correctly, and having to make the bed with corners tucked, but what I realized pretty quickly was that I liked having people to look up to in my first year, and I liked then becoming the person people looked up to in my third year—always wondering what rank I would end up with as my final rank . . . chasing a future self.

My two sides couldn't have been more different. On one hand I'm this free-flowing wild child who's in touch with her breath and would be happy to live in a sheet and out of a van, and then there's this other side of me that likes to be in a room making decisions, getting things done, and going 10 000 miles a minute. What I've found over the years, as I've experimented with trying to be just one part of me, is that it's impossible to do. And to be good at what I do I have to marry the two together because I can't lead without all of me. When we're in high-stakes conversations and feeling the pressure, what we do is lose access to the relaxed parts of ourselves, the hiking you, biking you, walking you, gardening you, jumping-in-the-waves you, the golfing you. This part of ourselves that we lose in these high-stakes situations is not only the logic and reason part but also the compassionate part, the seeing others as human part (Missimer 2020). One of the easiest ways to pause and reconnect to our whole self in jarring moments is through the breath.

We take about

- 12–18 breaths per minute
- 960 breaths an hour
- 17 000–23 000 breaths in a day
- 8 409 600 breaths in one year

And if we live to 80 years old, we're looking at taking about 672 768 000 breaths in our lifetime (Clare n.d.). You want to guess what happens when we're in stressful situations? Our breathing patterns change, and we can sometimes stop breathing or we breathe faster, shallower, from the chest, so we're not getting as much oxygen to the brain (Cox 2022) and not breathing out as much carbon dioxide. Our blood pressure rises, and we're in total fight, flight, freeze land where we've completely lost control of ourselves at the moment. More and more studies are showing how breathing interventions reduce stress and feelings of anxiety, as well as lower blood pressure, and can help control panic attacks (Bentley et al. 2023). And panic and stress is what's happening in the body during fired-up conversations.

In this chapter we'll get into why this practice works, and then I'll share some common breathing patterns that naturally happen during stressful conversations, and after that we'll move into specific breathing practices to combat our natural patterns so we can pause and reclaim our whole self in difficult situations.

Why Does This Practice Work?

When there was free time at Camp Tanamakoon I would walk the dirt paths and find my way through some bushes to this one rock on the side of the lake. It was the perfect height and size, where my feet touched the raised tree root at just a right angle. I would sit there and look out at Algonquin Lake. This was and still is, in my mind, my happy place. What I loved about this spot was watching the water move, seeing the different ways it would flow around obstacles, where it would get stuck and how it would make its way through whatever was in its orbit. And it did so with a gentle and friendly touch. The lake itself holds abundance within it, rocks, branches, mud, life, and while it's in constant motion, it's directed, focused. I think of the breath like I do the river. It's constant and can move through strong emotions, difficult thoughts, and uncomfortable sensations without being ruthless. When it's flowing easily it settles the chaos within by directing it, softening it, calming it, stabilizing it. By interrupting our usual reactivity with intentional breathing, our nervous system is able to still for a moment so that we can swerve past any swells that we could get caught up in.

Remember the vagus nerve from Chapter 4? This is the main nerve in the body that helps us move into our parasympathetic nervous system, or the relaxation response.[1] When we're in heated situations most of us either hold our breath or begin to breathe faster, which stops the vagus nerve from engaging. Along with touch, which we covered earlier, another way to bring the vagus nerve easily back online is with the breath. As we start to use practices to slow our breathing down, the vagus nerve picks up the cue of safety, and the body knows it can drop its armor. There have been many studies over the years showing how voluntary diaphragmatic breathing results in psychological flexibility and has a relaxing effect of lower blood pressure, reduced heart rate, less feelings of anxiety, and it also helps to control panic attacks (Zaccaro 2018, Hopper et al. 2019, Zou et al. 2017, Cowley and

---

[1] Herbert Benson coined the term "The Relaxation Response."

Roy-Byrne 1987). Diaphragmatic breathing is an umbrella term that consists of different types of paced breathing practices.

Frida was having a hard time connecting with one of her clients who had different political views than her. Anytime this client shared her opinions, Frida couldn't help but become agitated and judgmental. She understood she was either going to have to let the client go or learn how to allow her client to share without her intervening or trying to fix or convince. What she'd been realizing is that it wasn't just with this client she was reacting, but with many of them. She knew that she needed to find ways to model more responsive and intentional communication to her team and for other new business prospects. After a few meetings, I introduced her to some breathing practices to try when with her client. Once she found the right one for her, she could sit across the table and bite her tongue on certain things, which made their meetings much easier to manage and more productive.

Common Stressful Breathing Patterns

An awareness of what's going on with us in tough moments is key to implementing these pause practices, and so I want to invite you to start paying attention to how you breathe at work, when you're in a meeting, negotiating, delivering difficult news or feedback. See whether you note any of the following common stressful breathing patterns (Farhi 1996). If you pinpoint ones you do, this is good news, because it means that the breathing strategies that come after this section may be a good go-to pause practice for you.

Chest Breathing

When something is jarring the first thing we do is brace ourselves in some way. The muscles tighten in the body, and often the upper body feels it the most. When we are startled by something someone says or by the way they're reacting we tend to breathe in and out of our chest and we do so rapidly, feeling tension in our upper back, shoulders, and neck. It's those moments where we want to speed up the other person so they get to the point, or when we're insistent on a subject and keep repeating the same thing to make sure it's understood, or if we're prone to interrupt others, this is when the chest breathing usually shows up.

Breath Grabbing

There are natural pauses within a breath. You have the inhalation, the pause at the top of the inhalation, the exhalation, and the pause at the end of the inhalation. Breath grabbing is when we rush the natural pauses or don't allow for them. This often happens when we finish someone else's sentences or cut them off to give our opinion.

Frozen Breathing

Some people love cold weather. They love skiing and snowboarding. Well, I'm not one of those people. Usually when I'm cold my body feels stiff, and it's hard for me to want to do much of anything. This is kind of like what frozen breathing looks like, you're breathing, but everything remains rigid and tight—almost as if you can't even tell you're breathing in the first place. This way of breathing happens when we hold our breaths within our conversations, when we want to get the interaction right or accomplish our goal. We move into frozen breathing when we feel fear within our conversations.

Do any of the above feel familiar to you? They may not, because this might be the first time you've actually thought about your breath in conversations. Over the next few days start to notice if you fall into one of the above breathing patterns. Then come back and replace it with a new one, which I'm going to outline for you below.

Sensation + Take a Breath = Pause

I never thought about my breath or was in touch with my breath until I was 31 years old. Up to that point I didn't even know I was breathing at all, I took it for granted as it was something that my body did on its own and I didn't have to control or think about. Though that all changed for me on February 16, 2011, when my first love passed away unexpectedly while kayaking down a river and got caught in a swell. The moment I found out, I was aware that I was breathing and that he wasn't. Suddenly my breath became important—it became everything. My breath meant that I was here, and from then on all I wanted was to become a steward of my breath. At that point, I didn't know the science behind it and how or why it helps our bodies function optimally and move through difficult moments; all I knew was that I wanted to feel it more and pay more attention to it because when I did I felt better. My breath is what brought me through my grief to the other side; it is something that calmed me when I thought I was for sure going to be eaten by the fear and sadness of it all; it is what took something so complicated to navigate and made it simpler, easier to maneuver.

Discovering the breath and learning how to use it and slow it down is a superpower, as it is what anchors you within tough situations and helps you to pause, reset, think clearly, and begin again. Below are breathing practices to reach for when you feel the discomfort within the body.

Belly Breathing (Tavoian and Craighead 2023)

What's neat about the breath is that we can move it around the body, and when we have it travel to different places it can help us relax. A great place to take the breath is into the belly. Why I like this one so much is because it takes you quickly out of your head and into your body. To understand it, you can take

a minute and lie down on your back. Go ahead . . . lie down.
Now put the book on your belly. Then on the inhale through
the nose watch the book go up, and on the exhale through the
mouth watch it fall. Weird, right? Try it for three breaths. If
you're having a hard time knowing whether you're doing it,
put one hand on your chest and another on your belly. What
you want is to make sure the chest is still and the belly is what
is moving. By moving our breath to our belly we're taking in
deeper breaths and bringing more oxygen to the body, which
pushes out that fight, flight, freeze response, and instead brings
on the relaxation response.

You can do this practice sitting down or standing up, which
means it's a great go-to during meetings, presentations, dinners,
speeches. I usually recommend doing three belly breaths, because
the second one is when you'll usually find your shoulders release
a bit and feel more relaxed, and then the third solidifies the feeling. You can play around with how many work best for you.

Back Breathing

When I found out the breath could move I never once
thought to bring it to the back of my body. So much of the time
we're living a life lived forward that it's easy to forget about the
back of our body altogether. How often do you think of your
back? Maybe when you wake up in the morning or after sitting
for a long time you're reminded that it's there, but what if you
thought more about the function of your back more often. Your
spine is what gives your body structure, it's what lets you bend to
pick up a pen or turn around to grab a file; it also protects your
spinal cord, which is your nervous system (UMMC 2003).

I learned this breath when I was in labor with my son. You
can have different types of contractions, and mine were in my
back—for those of you who have gone through it, I'm happy
you got to the other side! Thankfully I had a doula with me,
who sat me down on a hard rocking chair and guided me to send

my breath toward my spine. This was my introduction to back breathing, and I've used it ever since.

It makes sense that when we breathe into the back we start to feel more relaxed, and things begin to slow down, and we feel a moment of rest because like I mentioned above, our nervous system is back here doing its thing. You can try it with me now. Put one hand on your back, for me it's easier if I put my palm facing up, or you can find a chair and scoot yourself all the way so your back is touching the frame. Now move your breath to where your hand is or where you feel the frame and inhale through the nose and see whether you can gently expand the back body, and then on the exhale let it fall. What helps most for me and my clients is to imagine that you are bringing the breath up the spine on the inhale all the way to between the shoulders and then follow the spine down on the exhale. Another way to do back breathing is to think of breathing into the bra line. You can do this practice either sitting down or standing up.

Breathing into the Feet

Leo had been diagnosed with ADHD, and while it helped him reach an executive level at his company, because he was passionate and hyper focused on the work he was doing, he found that during meetings in this new role, he was having a really difficult time paying attention. And when he was asked questions about his thoughts on the topic at hand, he was getting argumentative, dodging them, because he was trying to cover up the fact that he was having a hard time in those moments focusing. He was feeling scattered and out of control.

When we're dysregulated it can be quite scary for us, because we are no longer driving the train, and it's as if our brain and body have been taken over by something greater that we can't tackle or fend off. When Leo started to pay attention to his body more in meetings he began to notice this sensation of being scattered and out of control, and when it would happen his feet would start moving more under the table and would position themselves away from those he was with more toward the door. We don't pay a lot of attention to our feet, though they can tell us a lot about what we're feeling in the moment by the direction they're pointing. When we're in a stressful interaction our feet are primed and ready to help us flee to safety. What Leo decided to try to help him pause and then refocus so he could be a part of the discussion was to breathe into his feet. He would start to notice the sensation and the position of his feet, and then he would redirect his feet toward whomever was talking and then move his breath to them.

To do this breath, you bring your attention to the soles of your feet. Once your attention is on the feet, start to breathe from the soles of the feet. You may still feel your breath at the belly or chest, and that's okay; what we're looking for is for you to move your attention to the feet and send the intention of breathing into them toward them—then there is a sensation of expanding and contracting that happens within the foot itself.

Lengthen the Exhale

During the pandemic and still now, many in high-up positions are caught handling employee absences at the last minute. Whether it's when a project is on a tight deadline or it's presentation day, when multiple employees are out, it can put the pressure on to problem solve and make the plan happen anyhow. We've all been through it these last few years within our businesses and have had to deal with multiple stressors, and those in the education field have really had to step up in a way maybe they didn't even know they could. One of my clients is the head of a preschool and the amount that she was juggling during COVID, with parents, kids, and employees, was overwhelming; even now just the other month, half of the teachers were out with the flu. The pressure coming from the top, the parents, and the employees could make anyone lose their cool. Whenever we would talk,

I thought of the movie *Waiting to Exhale*. I've never seen the movie, so I don't know what it's about, but it's quite a catchy title.

There was always something on fire, and when that's the case, we're usually in the fight, flight, freeze breath, which is more rapid breathing, where we take more inhales than exhales. What worked really well for her was after noticing the emotional overload in her body, to focus on the exhale more than the inhale. So she would inhale at her regular speed and then extend the exhale, following it all the way to the natural pause at the end. If you feel that you're grasping for your next breath, then don't extend the exhale as long. The exhale is what softens not only the body, but also the moment.

Most of us focus more on the inhale, though the inhale is what activates the sympathetic nervous system (the fight, flight, freeze response), while the exhale moves us into the parasympathetic part of our nervous system, which is what we're trying to access within tough situations.

Finger Push Breathing

The philosopher Aldous Huxley said that "it's embarrassing that after 45 years of research and study, the best advice I can give to people is to be a little kinder to each other." While it's great advice, right now we all need a bit of help figuring out how to be kinder to one another within stressful interactions. To reach the place within a conversation where you can look at the person or group of people in front of you with compassion even if you don't agree with them requires that you give yourself a break within the interaction so that you can access clarity again. We get so caught up that we lose our logic within our conversations and instead act more emotionally, so to move ourselves back to seeing what is, finger push breathing can be a great practice.

The rhythm of this breath reminds me of ballet teachers who during exercises count to eight while snapping their fingers. You inhale while pushing your fingers down on a surface from your thumb to your pinky, and then you exhale while pushing your pinky to your thumb. You can also add counting as well, so on the inhale, beginning with the thumb it goes 1, 2, 3, 4, 5 and then on the exhale from your pinky to your thumb, you count 6, 7, 8, 9, 10. You can do this at a desk or a table, or you can even use your thigh. Note that the pushing isn't a big movement; think of it more like a quiet movement than an actual tap. I've been in conversations before where the other person was tapping visibly on the table, and all it did was make for an unpleasant interaction all around.

Left Nostril Breathing

As I started listening to my body more after my first love passed away, it was clear that at the time, I wasn't craving hard-core physical activity. Where before I would run, maybe lift some weights, all my body wanted now was gentle movement. This is also something my clients notice too, that the more stressful their working lives become, the more they need their activity level to release it. While sweating definitely helps, the other is more meditative movement, like yoga. What most people like about yoga isn't necessarily the postures; it's more the breathing and shivasana at the end. Yogic breathing is called pranayama. and studies show that it helps to reduce blood pressure and stress levels (Bargal et al. 2022). While whipping out a yoga pose would be taking it too far, what you can incorporate, kind of on the sly, is a bit of left nostril breathing. This type of breathing cools the body down in heated situations.

To do this breath, you close the right nostril and breathe through only the left nostril. You can do this for two to three cycles, and you'll feel yourself soften. This one can only be done while you're seated. You can either have your elbow on the desk and then your thumb under your chin and your pointer finger bent so the knuckle closes the nostril, or you can cup your chin, and your thumb rests gently under the nostril; you could also lean back in a chair, your left arms crossed over the body and the right elbow resting on the left, while your thumb is under your chin and your pointer finger is bent so the knuckle closes the nostril. To me the setup for this breath looks like the Auguste Rodin sculpture *The Thinker*. *The Thinker* is most often an image used to represent philosophy, as the figure is bent over with his hand under his chin in deep contemplation. Some believe it is a representation of the poet Dante Alighieri reflecting and meditating on the circles of hell in *The Divine Comedy*. Not saying our interactions go this deep in these difficult moments, but we are trying to pause to transcend our sometimes unskillful nature.

Breath Pattern

When you think of the last interactions or situations you've been in where it was difficult to pause, did it all feel it happened too fast? Where you got caught in the speed of the moment? The question everyone I work with asks is, how do I slow it all down? It's like what Rilke said, "Fundamentally, life requires us to yield to its 'velocity' if we want to partake of what it can offer." If we want to move through these high-stakes conversations easily, we have to yield to their velocity.

Stacey was part of a family-owned business. And when it comes to family businesses what's tough about it is that you have the personal and familial along with the bottom lines. There's a different kind of pressure within these types of organizations, as a lot of the identity of the company is embedded within the family itself. While the roles within the company were clear, the issue was that some of her siblings weren't pulling their weight. She would get really upset with her brother and sister because it felt as if they weren't as dedicated to the company as she was. Instead of being able to talk about it, the meetings would end with either yelling or one of them walking out the door. Nothing ever got resolved, and so this type of explosion happened at least once a month, which wasn't good for them or those that worked for them. She wanted to be able to sit in the room while emotions were high and be able to listen. For Stacey the sensation that would come was nausea in her stomach, and her jaw would clench. So the next time they all came together, sure enough, it came down to this same issue, and she felt the queasiness and the clenching of her jaw, and she knew it was time to soften and stay in the room. While her siblings kept talking and arguing, she yielded, by counting her breaths. Inhaling for five, holding for five, exhaling for five, until she felt her fists open. It didn't take long for her to do this, pause, see clearly, and listen to what they were actually saying, which changed the trajectory of the conversation because they were now feeling heard.

A breath pattern is a certain number of inhales and exhales, and there's usually a hold of the breath as well. The following are the two breath patterns I usually recommend to clients when beginning with this work.

Four-Part Breath Pattern

Inhale through the nose. Exhale through the nose. Inhale through the mouth. Exhale through the mouth. Inhale through the nose. Exhale through the mouth. Inhale through the mouth. Exhale through the nose.

This one you'll want to practice before doing it within an interaction so it comes naturally to you to do. A good time to practice is before going to bed at night or before a meeting and presentation. If you mess up on the pattern, that means you want to slow down the breathing itself. Slow it down so you get it right.

Five-Part Breath Pattern

You inhale for five. Hold for five. Exhale for five. When we do an equal part inhale, hold, and exhale we're creating a sense of balance within the body. Another pattern you can do is inhale for five, hold for one, and then exhale for six. The five-one-six pattern has more of a focus on the exhale, which means it's more of a relaxing breath.

Learning how to work with the breath, and redirect it, change its location, length, and fullness, changes our relationship to the tense situation we're in. When we learn to navigate the breath, we learn to pause and choose a more intentional way of connecting.

Make a Commitment

What are three practices that stand out to you? Or what three practices do you think would be the easiest to implement?

Write them down now.

1. _____

2. _____

3. _____

Choose one practice to try.

_____

CHAPTER

7

Eyes Toward Another

Not everyone is gonna think I'm funny or pretty, and that's okay. They're wrong though.

—Anonymous

Most of us who have worked hard to be in a leadership position have gotten here based on the choices and difficult decisions we've made. And sometimes it's easy to think we have all the answers and the way we do things is the right and best way. It's okay to admit it, at least to yourself. And know this, while it may not be the nicest thing to do, it's normal for us to make judgments of others and think of ourselves as better than. In psychology it's called superiority illusion: the belief that you are better than average in any particular metric (Yamada et al. 2013). In general, anyone who makes a decision that is backed by a thought believes the decision is correct and ideal. This means that everyone in your C-suite or your office or team feels this way. If you take a quick look on Reddit, you'll see posts upon posts from employees talking about how much more they know than those they work for. It's everywhere. We all have it within us, and usually we can keep a lid on it, but when there's a way you want something to be done and it doesn't match the way another person wants it to be done, then phrases such as "Idiot" or "This guy is just ridiculous" seep through the lips. This superiority illusion is what makes it hard to listen to others without getting riled up in some way.

We aren't ever going to stop disagreeing with people. And because of this superiority illusion it will always be that the other person doesn't know what they're talking about, because when we believe what we believe we're certain of it. There aren't any cracks or natural openings to let any other opinion in, and we're ready to defend and dodge and dance to make it so. As mentioned before, we harden to protect ourselves. As we make ourselves solid, we turn into walls, barriers, and shields. We become like the operculum of sea snails, like a trap door that keeps the soft part of the snail safe inside when it's threatened out of water.

It is our psychology that sets us up to separate ourselves into "it's not me; it's you." This belief that we are better and know more than others and inanimate objects (think of arguing with a traffic camera or your GPS) is what the majority of us are walking around thinking, believing, and then sharing in tone or verbally in difficult situations. This is what I like to call the "stupor of specialness." And what it creates is separateness, a way of dehumanizing others.

In most of our meetings and gatherings and calls during the day, we don't see each other as human, with hopes and dreams and fears and struggles; instead, we see each other as a threat to our specialness and to our very survival and bottom line. If we could soften toward others in heated moments, it could change the way we do business. Think of the different ideas that could be gathered, the strategies that could be entertained, the inspiration and excitement at the feeling of doing something together. This is what this pause practice is all about: turning toward those we're in the room with instead of away from them.

In this chapter I'll share more about why this practice works and then get into the hands-on strategies you can start to try out now.

Why Does This Work?

It was the last question of an already 75-minute long town hall, and Andi Owen, the CEO of MillerKnoll, the big furniture company, gave an 80-second response that went viral, and not in a good way. The question was about end-of-year bonuses, and the short clip shows her telling the employees to stop asking about the damn bonuses. "Spend your time and effort thinking about the $26 million that we need and not thinking about what are you gonna do if we don't get a bonus." If you watch the clip, you can see her frustration growing and growing, and the stupor of specialness rising and rising—what may have been meant to be motivational was now more of an attack. There's not one moment where she pauses, takes stock of the question or situation, the people she's talking to, and skillfully connects; instead, it's all biology talking. You can see she has no control over what she's saying; it's all her nervous system that leads her into a rant. This isn't the only instance of this; if you do a Google search, you'll see plenty of CEO temper tantrums as they're being called in the media. There's a lot right now circulating about how those at the top are out of touch with those in their companies, and it's more what's happening is there's a lack of oneness within organizations, a sense of community, togetherness. We still view business as a top-down structure, when more and more the true need is a roundtable, where everyone can see everyone else, sit next to each other, and come together with a shared purpose and goal, like Native American councils and communication circles.

Native American Communication Circles

Talking Circles originated with First Nations leaders—the process was used to ensure that all leaders in the tribal council were heard, and that those who were speaking were not interrupted (First Nations n.d.). Everyone sits around a table or in a circle, and whomever has the talking stick or feather is the one talking, while the others are listening. You can only talk when you have the talking stick, or you can choose not to talk and pass the stick. The stick is passed around in a clockwise direction, and what is said in the circle stays in the circle. Once everyone has spoken, the circle is finished.

You already know what makes a great leader—heck, you've likely bought book upon book to help inspire you, and over the years you've listened to your mentors, experienced, failed, learned, and started again, so it's not that you don't already know how important it is to hear and see those on your team, but what you might not have thought of before is how by doing that, it creates an environment where you and others want to come to work, show up, and put in the time and effort to help move the company along or the mission forward. At the end of the day, it helps to remember that you have chosen a role of service, and doing so requires that you stay connected to the core of it, the people with whom you work, especially in the defining difficult moments.

Again, we know that being skillful in these stressful situations doesn't come to us naturally; this isn't how we're wired, which is why the easy route in tough situations is to go off instinct and see our teams or those we work with as the other. With instinct there's no purpose behind our words, no intention or direction, and often they become useless because they aren't helping the situation; instead, they're creating more of a gap, divide, that makes it more difficult to mend. When we turn away from others in these moments, and we harden our shell, the issue remains. When we turn toward others we're showing that we want to connect on this challenge together, and when we connect, we create a bond, and when we have a bond with someone, we want to care for it, nurture it, and want the best for it. Bonds make us feel safe (Proges 2022, Schreiber 2023). When you find the bond, you find the pause. Think of everyone you work with like a plant or flower in your garden; you want to water them all, give them plenty of sunlight because if you ignore them, don't pay attention to them, well, the garden is no longer thriving. And the most important time to pay attention to them is when they're doing something different than what they're supposed to do or we feel they should do.

If we want those we work with to feel seen and heard, and we want to continue to grow within a company, then we have to start pausing so we can move ourselves out of seeing questions and ideas and thoughts as direct threats or difficult conversations as things to avoid. Shifting how you see someone in the moment moves you out of fight, flight, freeze, and into feeling more calm and connected; it's what creates the pause in a tense situation. Moving from "ugh" to "oh" or "not now" to "tell me more" is what we're after here.

It's a wonderful feeling when you walk into a place and feel a sense of camaraderie, where the space itself feels open, inviting, and comfortable. This feeling of comfort is what creates more relaxed interactions, more efficient and productive conversations, and a higher success rate (Khorrami 2020). The sense of safety within a conversation is what we're trying to get back to in these high-stakes conversations, and seeing the other person with friendly eyes gives that to us.

My therapist told me a story of how one day on the subway this big man came and sat down next to her. With his legs sprawled open he took up a lot of space. She said to herself, "Look at this guy; who does he think he is? Taking up so much space?" All these judgments started circling in her head—that something was wrong with him. And then, something happened. The man started singing "Over the Rainbow." As he started singing, my therapist decided to join him. And in that moment, all the separation dissolved, and there they were, two people, singing the same song. When it was her stop, she got up and turned toward him. "You made my day," she said, and he said, "No, ma'am, you made mine."

I love this story for countless reasons, and one of them is that it really shows how quickly separateness can dissolve, how turning toward someone can change the tone of the situation. Yes, we're hardwired to judge, protect, and react, which puts the barriers in place, yet what we're also wired for is connection, which is what we crave most, especially during a disagreement. What we're really looking for is reciprocity. We all want an "over the rainbow" moment in every tough situation we have, and these pause practices that are coming up next will show you how to get it.

Sensation + Turn Toward Another = Pause

Andy was a consultant who was brought into a company to help get it back on track. Doing this required him to make a lot of difficult decisions and have many hard conversations with a lot of people he didn't agree with. He was this new face coming in, and through other people's eyes it was always a feeling of who's this guy, coming in, thinking he knows how to run the show. He understood the situation and how awkward it was for a company that had been around for years to suddenly have him walk in and change the way things had been going so he could keep the business running and afloat beyond the year. It wasn't an easy situation for either party, and the challenge was that both Andy and the other company members were at odds on a lot of the ways things should go moving forward. Usually, Andy is an open and friendly kind of guy; he's energetic and likeable, which is why this position suits him, but the last few meetings he'd been in had him looking across the table thinking, *These guys don't know anything; they have no idea what they're talking about*. While they all were supposed to be on the same team, with the same goal, of keeping the doors open, they were ripping each other apart, making it harder and harder for anything to get done or changes to be made. It was even going so far as him and others hanging up on each other during phone calls.

With enough of these instances under his belt, it quickly became a me-versus-them mentality, which had him on edge. He couldn't control it anymore. Any email that came through, *These idiots*, he'd say, and the minute the doors were closed he was ready to spar. It went on like this for months, until he decided to do something different. What he did was try on some of the following pause practices to see whether he could find space within these moments to change the way he was seeing those he was now working with—to pause. And when he did, there was movement again, little by little the room was being heard, and agreements and compromises were on the table.

If you're experiencing something similar, the following pause practices may be the ones for you to try on.

Ask Yourself Questions

When I was a little kid I remember the moments where I would hit my leg on a table or fall down, and the adult with me would say, "What did that table do to you?" It really was my first introduction to this idea that I could blame something for what was happening. And it was easy to do. If something didn't work out, it was the other person's fault. Blame has no place within business, because the moment we get stuck in who did this, or they did that, we've lost our goal, purpose, momentum; we're stuck in the mud, and wheels are spinning because we aren't taking any responsibility for what's happening; we forget that we have a role in what's going on and that we can change our role at anytime. When we're in uncomfortable situations, whether we realize it or not, we're already blaming—*Who do they think they are? They have no idea what they're talking about; they're making a mountain out of a molehill; if they would just relax, listen.* They, they, they are the problem.

When you experience the cue of discomfort in the body, the finger is usually pointed at the other person and what they're doing that's wrong. It's the old anonymous saying of "*When a man points a finger at someone else, he should remember that three of his fingers are pointing at himself.*" This isn't to be used in this context as a "look at what you're doing" type of thing; it's more a reminder that when the unpleasant sensation comes in the body, our attention is on the wrong thing. To get the moment back in alignment, to pause, and begin again, we move our attention and redirect it to asking ourselves questions.

Choose one or a few of the following questions to silently ask yourself while in the difficult situation and see how it softens the moment, creates a pause and allows for discussion.

- How can I be helpful to this person right now?
- How can I be supportive of this person's thoughts and ideas right now?
- How can I listen the whole way through?
- How can I be kind right now?

- How can I see them with friendly eyes?
- What do we have in common right now?
- Can I acknowledge the other person's needs, fears, frustrations?
- Who am I talking to? Why do they need what they need?
- What can I do?
- What is possible?
- Is there a way I can align with my team right now?

When we start to ask ourselves questions during heated conversations we pause and start to see the person in front of us as someone we care for, respect, want to hear from, and continue to work with.

Compassion Power

We had been in our new house a couple of weeks when walking by our neighbors' house I noticed a stone embedded within the cement. It was a beautiful rose rock cut in the shape of a heart. The next morning before getting the kids into the car, I told them that we were going to get compassion power for the day. My kids are young, so when they asked what compassion power was, I said, "It's being kind to ourselves and others." Though compassion power is more than that. Most of us think that compassion is about being kind, and that's a part of it, but it's really about being able to see our own discomfort and the discomfort of others and hold space for it and to help alleviate it.

Can we be with our own discomfort within a conversation without blame, resentment, or other fear-based behavior? Can we accept and allow the anger and irritation and annoyance and frustration that we feel, and can we also accept and allow the other person or group of people's anger, irritation, and annoyance and frustration as well? Without judgment and evaluation? This is what compassion power looks like within a disagreement. Can you sit next to the discomfort in the room instead of becoming it?

The moment the unpleasant sensation comes that usually pushes us into our default reactions of raising our voice, getting angry and defensive, becoming rude and dismissive is when we have to do the opposite. So rather than withdrawing our kindness, openness, accessibility, can we offer it instead?

One way to cultivate compassion toward the other within an interaction is by silently reciting phrases that you'd find within a loving kindness or metta meditation. Metta meditation is a formal seated meditation practice, though for this, we aren't using it in its formal form; we're using it more as a mindfulness practice, to access the pause and soften within the moment. What's wonderful about formal meditation practices is that almost all of the different types of meditations can be used actively, in short form, within daily situations to help us turn on the rest and relaxation within our bodies in stressful situations. This specific formal meditation is often used to help people feel more connected to themselves, others, those they're having difficulty with, and the world at large. It's a go-to meditation for those times we may be feeling helpless and stuck, which is why when we pull phrases from it and use it in its short form it's great in high pressure situations because it takes our focus off the problem and instead gives us a moment, a pause, a new way of seeing the other person or group of people in front of us so we can find a new path to go down.

There are a lot of different phrases people use with this meditation. Over the years I've played around with many different ones, and I've landed on some that really resonate with me and help me to soften. I invite you to try mine out and see whether any of them feel right for you; if they don't, then feel free to come up with your own. Remember, these practices I'm sharing with you here are strategies that not only work for me but also for those I work with, and what happens with them is that they're yours, which means you take them and morph them into what works best for you. Here are the silent phrases I say to myself that help me pause and change the way I'm seeing the person in front of me.

- May you know love.
- May you know joy.
- May you know peace.
- May you be free from suffering.
- May you live with ease.

If there's one in the above list that feels good for you, take it and start trying it out. If none of them seem your style, then you're going to take a moment and think what you want for those you work with, what do you wish for them, or hope for them. This is for you to start turning them back into humans, with wants, needs, feelings, dreams, and fears in the moments they suddenly become the enemy. If you're having problems finding phrases, what helps me is thinking about what you want for yourself, and then you offer those same wants for others. You won't recite all of these within a high-stakes situation, but you can pick one and repeat it, or you can take max three to try out.

Appreciation

It was tax time this past week, and I've waited for hours on the phone to get through to DC Tax and Government. They were experiencing a high volume of calls, which left the wait time to 57 minutes. On Monday I waited an hour and then had to drop for a work call. On Tuesday I waited two hours and then had to drop for a work call. On Wednesday I waited 20 minutes and then had to drop for a work call. On Thursday I waited an hour, and they gave me the option for a call back, and when they called back, two hours later, I was on a work call!

So, today, I called at 8:45 a.m., put my callback number in, and at 12 p.m. my phone rang. I was so happy to talk with Gerri on the other end of the line. And you know what? It was worth the wait. Why? (i) Because I was deeply thankful to be talking to her, and (ii) Gerri was exceptionally kind and helpful. I could tell she was smiling through the phone. Up to this point I don't know how many people she had already talked to, but I let her know she was worth the wait.

Before I knew how to soften and turn toward the other person I didn't approach these kinds of situations the same way. Before I would have been really annoyed and frustrated, I would have thought I was owed better service, because it's my tax dollars at work, I would have let it ruin my day or be something I dwelled on and let everybody know about. And then when I would finally connect with someone, I would be angry at them and mean. When I started to bring appreciation into my conversations, I was able to pause—see then that this person wasn't put here to upset me, it wasn't their intention to make things hard for me, they were actually there to make my life easier, to answer the questions I had, and if I saw them through this lens, what was stressful was no longer that. This is the same as in business, everybody that's working with you, for you, or the deals you're making or the clients you're entertaining, the talks you're giving, the development and growth that's happening or the building stages that you're in, all of these people in your day-to-day are here to make your work, your days more than instead of less than. Even a good debate or disagreement can be done from an appreciative stance.

A stance of appreciation within tough situations is a game changer. It decreases our heart rate, helps us regulate, and also motivates us (Khorrami 2020). When we feel appreciative of the person we're with, we pause in acknowledgment of what they're doing or trying to do for themselves, their team, and how they're doing it, the courage with which they're doing it; or we pause by reminding ourselves of their abilities, the time put in, and loyalty, and help they provide.

Try It Now

In the white space of the book or if you have a place to write, take a minute and think about the people you usually get into it with in your office or those from other companies you're working with, etc. Write down their names, and underneath highlight three things you appreciate about this person. Do you feel a shift in how you see them? Before the next meeting, phone call, big day, get into the stance of appreciation, jot down one or two things you appreciate, and then when you feel the unpleasant sensation remind yourself of them to soften and pause.

Relax Your Eyes

I was 10 when I found out I saw the world differently than other people. While everyone saw one of everything, I saw double. Two of you, two of me, the world was a very cluttered place. And once it came to light, my mother got me involved in vision therapy, and I trained my eyes to see one—one point of focus, one direction, one way to go. This one way was the way for me until I was instructed in one of my meditation practices to keep my eyes open, look a few inches in front of me, and let my eyes see everything. I was told not to focus on one thing in particular, not to give too much attention to any one thing, let everything feel the same. When I let it happen, my eyes felt relaxed, and I could see everything. It wasn't only the cushion in front of me, but it was all of the cushions, all of the people, all of the windows, all of the walls, the doors. The moments when I feel the unpleasant sensation rising in my body is when I know I'm fixated or looking too hard in one direction; it's really tunnel vision, only seeing what's in front of me. When we have this hard stare is when we again find ourselves attached and trapped in the tentacles of the conversation. It's quite relaxing to let your eyes rest for a minute from an angered or scolding stare.

Try It Now

It's a quick little exercise, but go ahead and stare hard at the text, or if you're listening in, find something to direct your eyes toward, and while you're doing it, notice your breath. Now soften the eyes, don't focus on any one thing in particular, and notice your breathing. Was anything different? Usually with a one-pointed focus our breathing is shallow, and its movement is more vertical. Then when you soften the eyes the breath naturally becomes wider within the body, and the breath is deeper, lower down into the belly.

We know from before that intense moments cause our bodies to breathe shallow and at a quick speed, and how we're looking at something directly reflects how we're breathing and taking in our surroundings. Either we're in a field, trying to get from point A to point B without being eaten, so we're in a heightened state, ready to pounce, or we're hanging out in a big field with no predators in sight, and we can take in the view and move slowly and calmly any place we'd like to go.

When we soften our gaze we start to see the other person or group of people in a more friendly way; they start to become people again, ones we're interested in knowing or learning more about. When we're in challenging moments it's very easy to see only one way, so when we feel the unpleasant sensation, we relax our eyes, pause, and then are able to open and connect in a way we weren't able to before.

Open Up

There has been some internal fighting going on within Justin's team at work. Most of the challenges are related to trust or the lack thereof with each other. While he wants his group to feel more cohesive, he can't help but overreact during their meetings when there's overlapping work that's being done because of the competitiveness and miscommunication. There have been times where he's walked out of a meeting or sent others out of the room because of feeling completely overwhelmed. This type of reaction can't continue for his work security or his teams. With everyone pulling him in different directions he was getting so caught up in the separateness and the chaos that he was creating more of it. When he started noticing his body in these moments he saw he was in more of an aggressive stance, his hands firmly on the table with his body leaning forward; sometimes he would start pointing his fingers, or without realizing, his hands would be in fists by his sides, or he'd stand up and pace around with his hands on his hips. These types of postures led to more disconnection, where those around him felt less than, uncomfortable, and at the ready to defend themselves or dismiss someone else to look better in his eyes, which is the opposite of what we need in these moments. When feeling these sensations in his body, he worked on using postures that showed he was interested, ready to listen, and open to connection instead of those that had him ready to be taken out by the next challenge.

Think of how your body is when you're welcoming someone into your home. You open the door for them, your body is open, turned toward them, which sends the signal not only to yourself that all is okay, but also to those walking in. A difficult meeting is no different, because the people within the space are your guests; you've invited them there to be with you today, or maybe you were invited to be there—either way, there's already an established sense of respect, community, and togetherness. Most of those on Justin's team felt for a long time that they were their own little island, completely isolated from him and each other. By relaxing his posture in these difficult meetings, he was able to pause and not only bring everybody onto the mainland but also help them off the boat with an open hand, reminding them that he had invited them.

A connected posture means your entire body is turned toward those you're speaking to, think whole body listening here (not just your head or your upper body—the lower half and feet as well!) You're upright but not uncomfortable—and it's a seat you respect and one that moves fluidly forward to show interest and engagement, and backward to show thought, acknowledgment, and possible understanding.

Fill the Bucket

My son shared with me the concept of filling someone's bucket. The idea is that we want to fill the buckets of those we care about because filling the bucket means we're making them feel good. In these tough conversations we aren't anywhere close to filling someone else's bucket; it's sitting there, clear as day, but we don't see it. We're in survival mode; we're in attack mode or an us-versus-them mode—who cares about a friggin' bucket? If, though, we want to start pausing in these intense moments so we can continue to keep and foster relationships with our teams, clients, investors, shareholders, or the board, then we have to start acknowledging that each person has a bucket with their name on it, and by seeing and acknowledging it when we feel that uncomfortable sensation in the body, we pause and then can decide how best to fill the buckets of those we're with in the moment.

In heated situations we're frustrated with the other person or group of people. We want them to understand the issue or the idea, we want them to see how the proposal fixes the challenge being faced, or we just don't understand how they can't see that this is the best way to get the deal to go through or the fairest terms we're going to get. We try so hard in these moments to change what's happening that we resist how things actually are. If we could in these moments pause and see, "Oh, this is what's happening right now, no one is relating to me and what I'm saying, I'm trying to get these people to listen and to hear me, and it's not working," and feel the anger and the irritation of that and the aggression building in the body, and then turn toward the others and pause, then collaboration, connection, and a sense of community can be created or continue.

Make a Commitment

What are three practices that stand out to you? Or what three practices do you think would be the easiest to implement?

Write them down now.

1. _____

2. _____

3. _____

Choose one practice to try.

_____

CHAPTER

8

Need to Say

Evidence is conclusive that your self-talk has a direct bearing on your performance.

—Zig Ziglar

We don't know it, because it's all happening so quickly, but the moment we feel that unpleasant sensation within us we're thinking something, telling ourselves something. And usually what we're telling ourselves is helping our bodies stay in their defensive mode, it's helping us continue to feel threatened and under attack. Either we're saying things to ourselves about ourselves that are hurtful or we're on a roll with unhelpful thoughts about those we're in the room with. The neat thing about our chemical makeup is that it all is here to help. If you were in a seriously dangerous situation these skeptical, judgmental, and apprehensive thoughts would be keeping you safe and protected; the problem, though, is in the office, these thoughts keep the body in a stressful state, which can move quickly into irrational behavior.

One of the biggest wants that people have when they start working with me is learning how to change their language during overwhelming moments. They want to learn how to say the right thing, to make sure the other person doesn't react or get hurt. I usually let people know off the bat that they're focusing on the wrong thing. The first and most important part is that they're saying the right thing to themselves so they can keep their cool in these situations. Once they do that, then the right words come intuitively.

There's a Grimms' fairy tale I read when I was younger that my kids have recently found called "The Magic Porridge Pot." It's about a mother and daughter who don't have anything to eat. And one day the daughter goes into the forest and meets an old woman who shows her a magic pot that when she says, "Cook, little pot, cook" the pot makes porridge, and when she says, "Stop, little pot, stop," the pot stops making porridge. The girl takes the pot back to her house, and she and her mother are now able to eat whenever they want. Then one day the girl goes out into town, and at home her mother says, "Cook, little pot, cook." And the pot starts making porridge. When the mother is full and ready to stop, she wants the pot to stop cooking, but she doesn't know the right words to say. Soon the porridge fills up the kitchen and then makes its way through the entire house and out of the door and into the village and it continues in this way until it reaches the last house where the little girl sees what's happening and says, "Stop, little pot, stop." With the right words the pot stops making porridge and the village is safe. It's the same in difficult situations: there are words and phrases we can use to help us feel safe in the moment so that we don't overflow and give over to our emotions that could jeopardize our positions, relationships, or a project or deal we've been working toward for a long time.

In this chapter I'll be showing words and phrases that help us stop our porridge pots from spilling over.

Why Does This Work?

Studies have shown that how we talk to ourselves can help us regulate our emotions (Bakker 2017). And while many have said it before—that by changing your thoughts and words you can change your life—what I've found is that when you say certain words and phrases to yourself in tough situations, you can change the state of your nervous system. By using certain words and phrases during high-stress situations, we can pause—reduce the stress response, our anxiety, and can feel more in control. In this context, we're using words and phrases as not only a pattern interrupter but also as a way to psychologically distance ourselves from the overwhelming sensation we're caught within.

In 2022, a study was done with tennis players (Fritsch et al. 2022) to see what the difference was between goal-directed self-talk and spontaneous self-talk. The goal was to see the relationship between self-talk and emotions. Twenty competitive tennis matches were recorded, and afterward the players were asked to look at the situations from the match and to rate the intensity of their emotions, reactions, and share about their self-talk. What they found was that the intensity of emotions experienced and the emotional reaction were lower when players reported only goal-directed self-talk. This is the self-talk we're looking for within high-pressure situations—goal-directed, intentional. We're not interested in what's usually milling about in our heads (spontaneously) during these times of difficulty; we want our language to help us move out of the heightened state we're in so we can bring ourselves back to calm and finish the meeting, town hall, session, you name it. An older study done in 2014 by psychologist Ethan Kross of the University of Michigan (Kross et al. 2014) showed that when people use their own name within their self-talk or talk to themselves in the second-person pronoun, you, it can help them to regulate their emotions, helping them change the way they feel and behave.

The self-directed talk we're going to be using is a mix of go-to words and phrases. The goal of these words isn't motivating talk like you'd see in sports, and it's not fandom talk either; the goal for us is to find words and phrases that relax the body, helping us create the moment that breaks the momentum of the interaction—the pause. What we're also after within this self-talk is more of a kind and friendly tone. Think back to a conversation when someone raised their voice at you, or maybe the volume wasn't loud, but the tone was deafening—how did it feel? Likely not good, because our bodies can quickly move into the stress response based on the tone of voice we hear.

Ready to dive in?

Sensation + Need to Say = Pause

Since the pandemic Martin's company has gone with the hybrid approach, so employees have to be in the office at least two days out of the week. It's something that he's still getting used to as he didn't grow up in this kind of working environment and is really used to seeing, talking face-to-face, and having that personal connection with those who work with him. The in-office days feel off because of the out-of-office days, and he's been finding it more difficult to keep his calm when he's disagreeing with someone on his team. He constantly resorts back to the same story in his mind that this wouldn't be happening if everyone were back in the office full-time as before. It's breeding mistrust and exclusion, and as he's been so quick to react that his team's dynamic is breaking down.

What's happening for Martin is quite common right now; there's overwhelming change with how people are working, and it's disrupted what once felt certain. Knowing how work gets done is something leaders have been studying since work began, but since the pandemic for lots of companies out there, it feels as if they were starting anew and writing their own playbook as they go. While entrepreneurs have that kind of "build a business on the way up" mentality, Martin wasn't an entrepreneur; he was someone who had been doing this work in the same kind of environment for more than twenty years. He felt stuck, and he knew that turning this around was imperative, as this was, at least for now, what the working world was looking more and more like. What he needed was to disrupt these spontaneous and unintentional outbursts, to pause, get unstuck and back to a place where he felt more at ease in the conversations over Zoom and in person. What the go-to words and phrases did was help him move out of the fear, anger, doubt, worry, and help him to quiet the mind and the body so he could pause and reconnect with his team and find a new way to work with them.

The phrases and words below have been helpful to me and those I work with, and I invite you to take what works for you here as well. I do want to stress that these aren't the only go-to phrases to use; you can use any word or phrase that helps you feel more calm and at rest in heightened moments, and I encourage anyone doing this work to play around and find what works best for them. You may want to take a minute and think whether there are any words or phrases you already use in your day-to-day that bring you back to balance. If so, see whether you can silently say one to yourself in the moment you feel the unpleasant sensation rising in the body, and see what changes.

One note here is the power of three. If you work in advertising, marketing, or branding, even sales, and have given talks, or done stand-up comedy, really it's everywhere—you've probably heard that saying things three times or grouping in three is the way to go. Why? Because our brain recognizes patterns, and the smallest kind is three (location, location, location; life, liberty, and the pursuit of happiness; 9 1 1; three blind mice), which makes it simple to remember and share. We use the power of three here, by saying the words shared below to ourselves three times. The power of three in this context is a pattern that helps the brain and the body touch a place of calm within us that helps to detach and separate from the emotional landslide we're facing.

Now, let's get into the words and phrases to help you pause, and we'll start with my favorite one.

Soften

I know, I know, you're probably tired of this word already, but I'm telling you it has incredible power! While SOFTEN is an acronym, and what you're learning how to do with each practice, it's also a word you can use in a high-stakes conversations to access the "rest and digest" part of your nervous system. This one really does remind me of *The Wizard of Oz* when Dorothy clicks her red shoes together saying, "I want to go home, I want to go home, I want to go home" (see the pattern of three?). The word "soften" takes you back to homeostasis in the body, and when you say it three times, you'll feel your shoulders start to relax and melt down the back, and you'll feel your breathing start to deepen and the exhale start to lengthen. It's not a rapid recitation of the word; it's a slow repeat of the word.

Try It Now

Say "soften" to yourself three times, and notice what happens within the body. Does anything feel different? Do any areas feel more relaxed? For me the "so" comes on the inhale, and the "fen" comes on the exhale—each person will find their own rhythm that works.

I know the word soften can put some people off, because it's not what we're taught to do or instinctively do in tough situations. These moments though are trust-building moments with your colleagues and your teams, and trust is a fragile thing, like an egg. So to keep it, we have to dissolve our stress response, and saying "soften" to ourselves in the moment is one practice to help us do it.

Swerve

David would be sitting in meetings listening to the information given to him, and he couldn't tell whether any of it was true or what was being left out. Over the years he found that employees would often say the good things and not share so much of what was really happening. There was always a lot of information given, though none of it felt meaningful or helpful. I liken it to a cappuccino; many meetings that leaders find themselves in are the foam—employees saying what they want management to hear, making things sound better than they are— and it's difficult to get under the foam and into the coffee. And that's what David tried to do in his meetings, but he wasn't getting anywhere with it. All he wanted to know was what was going on within the company, and while he wanted a candid response, he was getting so caught up in the moment that he was becoming patronizing, dismissive, and shaking his head a lot with passive-aggressive sighs, thinking, *Just tell me what's going on, somebody*.

I've mentioned before that in these moments our attention is on the wrong thing. We're so focused on what the other people are or are not saying and doing that we get caught in the moment, so it's hard to stop ourselves from overreacting. Instead we want to swerve. Swerve around the net trying to catch us, swerve past the language of the other person, swerve and go another direction. This word gives us the moment we need to pause and change our direction within the conversation. Over the next few meetings David was swerving over and over and again, and as he felt that he was creating a bit more space between the stimulus and the response, he was starting to brainstorm other ways, besides within his meetings, to find the truth about what was happening within the company. He started to change his approach, by going out for a run with his employees once a month. This change-up brought a new level of trust and connection to those relationships.

Open

I've been talking a lot about the leaders who react in stressful moments by getting louder, being more aggressive, dismissive and argumentative, or passive-aggressive, though there is also the one who gets extremely quiet in more difficult situations, where the body goes into the freeze mode and everything shuts down. This is Hillary. She has gotten to where she is in her career because she is the person who says yes to everything, and others know she will get it done without talking back, questioning, or ruffling the feathers at any point along the way. Easygoing is how many would describe her. Though what most people don't realize is that easygoing in these types of situations is a stress response. We become the yes person out of fear—we want to be liked, we don't handle confrontation well, we hate to mess up or make a mistake—so it's easier to stay quiet because then the likelihood that we'll make a mess is slim. Now, though, Hillary is leading a team, and she wants her team to like her so when someone who isn't holding up their weight asks her how they are doing, she can't answer honestly; instead, she freezes, unable to give critical or helpful feedback. In these moments, she closes up shop and exits out the window. Ninety percent of employees say they want honesty and integrity from their managers, but when our nervous system puts us in freeze mode, all of that is on the other side of the window.

Hillary closes down when the unpleasant sensation is happening in her body, and what needs to happen is the opposite—to open. During these conversations where she is being asked to give feedback or share a difficult decision or say no to one of her employees she can feel the tightness in her chest and the nausea in her stomach and say to herself, *Hillary, stay open, open, open.* Saying this word three times changes the breath of the body to a wide, full-body breath, relaxes the shoulders back and down, changing the stance of the body, and reminds us that fear is not in control of the moment, but we are.

Disengage

Remember when I mentioned I'd gotten my yellow belt? Well, there was a period in my life where I really wanted to learn self-defense, and I had remembered an ex-boyfriend had practiced akido, so I decided to find a studio near me and start. I'm rather small, five feet two, five feet three on good days, and in one of the first classes I was paired with a rather large and tall guy. He was supposed to grab me, and I was supposed to find my way out of the hold. Instinctively I fought back, I wiggled, struggled, tried thrashing my legs side to side, but nothing worked. Then the instructor taught us to drop our weight, to completely disengage from the situation itself, to soften the body completely. The moment I did this I was out of his grasp in seconds. The former president and CEO of PayPal Dan Schulman talks about how martial arts has helped him within his leadership roles, by teaching him practices to keep calm in a crisis (Rutgers 2018). What it taught me was this idea of disengaging from intense situations, showing me how to let go so I wouldn't be dragged. Instead of giving over to the body's natural response in difficult conversations, we unplug from them.

With the overcharged interactions and situations we can find ourselves in, it's that moment where we can step out of its grip that makes all the difference. A word that has helped a lot of clients in the height of a moment is "disengage." The word helps us to stop struggling and fighting and instead lets us let go of the situation we may be holding on too tightly to. When I say, "Cynthia, disengage, disengage, disengage," I feel as if I were a spaceship coming back to earth, and it's the moment when the parachute opens, and I'm floating, breathing, and giving myself the opportunity to land safely.

Reset

Joanne is the head of business development within her company, and she's noticed that it's difficult for her team to engage with new clients intuitively; they often rely on a script or notes. Each time she hears about a lost opportunity or a possible sale walking out the door, she snaps and launches into hurtful language that demoralizes the team. She's often leaving these meetings feeling she should have done more to understand their point of view and what's really going on that's making these connections so hard to follow through. *Why can't they just do their jobs? It really isn't that hard to do.* We've all had moments, like Joanne, where we'd like to have a do-over—I know I've had plenty—so before we get to that place, where we're feeling self-conscious about how we've interacted and we have to go and repair the situations, what we can do is reset within the conversation itself.

If you've ever played Nintendo with the original game console, resetting is the moment where, during play, you have to take the game out, blow into it, clear it from the dust, and put it back in so it starts working again. That's what we're doing in these hard situations, clearing the dust that's blurring our vision and upsetting our nervous system. When you start to feel the unpleasant sensation rushing in the body, you can say to yourself, *[Your name], it's time to reset,* or *It's best to reset, reset, reset.*

Clear

There was a period of extreme anxiety for me in my business, where my mind wouldn't stop moving from one worry to the next. Usually it was about my team, as I really wanted to make it all work for them—to pay them well, to be transparent and accessible to them, to have this happy family. And when some people weren't happy, I was so fixated on trying to fix and tend to the problems and challenges that I stopped enjoying what I was doing and what I had created in the first place. My relationship with my team started to falter because I was putting their needs above my own, and this started to affect my conversations. A teacher of mine, Pratima, suggested I sit with my eyes closed, and whenever a negative thought or anger- and fear-based thought came, to say the word "clear." And when I would do this I felt as if I were back in the Duck Hunt Nintendo game I had as a kid—or what I imagine clay shooting to be like. And over time I was saying "clear" less and less.

I took this lesson over into high-stakes conversations, and it works the same. The difference is that it's when you feel the sensation rising in the body that you say the word "clear." And it's not meant to be used in such a direct and forceful way—like I imagined it with the Duck Hunt. Here it's more like when you're at the beach, and you write your name in the sand, and the waves come up and clear it away. It's that image to think on when you say the word—a kind of clearing away, watching it sail away. For me what works well is exhaling when I say the word "clear," seeing the waves move away from the shore, and on the inhale seeing the waves come into the shore, and again saying to myself "clear" on the exhale and watching the waves move away.

Can I Make This Feel Like a Little Deal?

I have a four-year-old girl and a six-year-old boy, and if you talk to my son, he will tell you that the idea for this book came from him. Why? Because he goes to this amazing camp called PowerPlay that teaches him how to regulate his emotions, and one of the tools is to use the pause button. What I love about children's curricula for emotional regulation (Unstuck and On Target) is not only the simplicity, making it easy to remember, but also the phrases used. One that we use a lot in our house is, "Is this a little deal or a big deal?" When you're my kids' ages you're learning whether when a piece of paper is ripped warrants the same reaction as if you fall down and crack your chin open, or if not having enough time to finish an activity you're excited about warrants the same reaction as someone being mean on the bus over and over again. While we're no longer taking school buses, most of us adults are still trying to decipher during the day what's a big deal that warrants a bigger reaction and what's a small deal that doesn't.

These tough situations we find ourselves in feel like really big deals. And, well, they are—some of these conversations are make-or-break for you and your family, the company, the people you work with, the economy and markets. Anytime you are in a heated conversation at work you are up against your very own survival within the organization—not only in finding a way to collaborate or problem solve and fix, but to do so without a red flag, in a way that can be trusted and done with integrity. I tell those I work with all the time, the reason it feels like a big deal to you is because it is a big deal. Now, here's the challenge, and here's the pause. Ready for it? *What we need to do is turn what feels like the most gigantic deal into a little deal.*

We can turn the emotional overload we feel in the moment, the sensation that heightens within us into something manageable that we can work with. To do this, we have to make it smaller.

After my dad climbed Mt. Kilimanjaro, he said the only way to get there was to do it pole by pole. The intensity of the situation changes when you notice the discomfort and say to yourself, *This feels like a big deal. How can I turn what feels like a big deal into a little deal?* Putting your name in front of it will help as well. In full honesty, I get overwhelmed quite easily, even going into a big grocery store can put me over the edge, and when I feel the chaos starting within, I say, *Cynthia, this feels like a big deal; how can you make it a little deal?* And just like that, my body softens, and I've given my system the reset it needs to face the fruits and vegetables aisle by aisle.

Back to Neutral

When I was growing up, one of my best friends drove a manual car. My favorite part was when we'd get to a stop light or stop sign and she'd move the stick to neutral and toggle it from side to side. In neutral it's completely detached from the gears and it would make this faint sound when she would shake it, making sure it was in the center position. What if we thought of our conversations more like a manual car? Right now tough situations and conversations are automatic, we have a way we react within them, and that's the pattern, not much to think about, except afterward when we've realized our behavior has affected our reputation, our bottom line, our teams, and the company. Manual means we're in control of the machine itself, not being led by it. To pause, this is what we're attempting to do, to start to be the one shifting the gears within a conversation instead of it being done for us. Just this afternoon, leaving my son's soccer game, we were behind a student driver, who was learning how to drive a manual car. It took him a while to get all the pieces together, the feet, the stick shift, and soon, the car started to sputter forward. Another stop sign and the same thing happened, he slowed down. Full stop. Took his time to figure out what to do, and then the car screeched forward. Each time before he began, he had to come back to neutral.

Neutral is the moment of rest we want to find in the body before, during, and after hard conversations. We all have this place of rest within the body at all times; it's just that we disconnect from it in the heat of an intense moment. What does rest feel like? It feels quiet and still. It's like when you look out in the morning at a body of water, and it seems like a sheet of glass.

Try It Now

Take a long, slow, deep breath, starting at the belly, and then move the breath up the chest and then the nostrils, and then let it travel back down and out the belly. Now bring your attention to the top of your head, and then direct your attention to the face, ears, throat, down the arms, chest, moving it all the way down the body. And while you're here, see if you can identify where rest lives in your body. It's the place inside that isn't buzzing with energy. And if you can't find it . . . don't worry, the more you start to implement some of the practices within the book, the easier it will be to find.

When we're in our stress response, we can pause by redirecting our attention to this place of rest in the body. And we can find it by reminding ourselves that it's there, saying to ourselves, *Back to neutral, can we get back to neutral, find neutral. Neutral, Neutral, Neutral.*

[Name], You're in Control

I'm around 11 or 12, and I'm riding in the car with my sister. My dad is taking us to Mansfield, Ohio, to try skiing for the first time. I am exhilarated because I've heard people talk about skiing and how much they love it, and now I get to try it. Once we get there, we put on layer after layer, and while I'm feeling a bit uncomfortable, I chalk it up to this is what people who ski do, so I'm doing it too. I don't remember there being a bunny hill we started on; what I do remember is how frightening it was to get onto the ski lift and then how exposed I felt on the ride up the mountain. When we reached the top I was so scared I wouldn't get off in time that I tripped over the person in front of me. I was a mess. Then, it was actually time to start skiing, and all I remember was barreling down this mountain unable to stop myself, scared I was going to hit somebody, hurt them, hurt me; *Would this ever end? Just get down the hill, Cynthia, you can do it*. I felt the most out of control I'd ever felt, and so when I got down to the bottom and ran into a log I was the happiest I'd ever been. The speed at which we go down a mountain is similar to the speed of disagreements. It's impossible when you're going that fast to know what's happening, think about anything clearly, choose how you want to interact, because all that you're feeling is adrenaline. What we need is a reminder in the moment that we are the ones in control, not our emotions.

What better way to remind ourselves of this than by telling it to ourselves in the moment it's happening. When you feel the unpleasant sensation rising in the body, say *[Your name], you're in control, you get to decide how to interact right now. [Your name], turn this into an opportunity to learn more*. What our emotion makes us forget within these high-stakes conversations is that we have a choice in how we show up within them. There is a constant power struggle going on within us, and when it gets tough our emotion and stress is louder than our calm and cool, which means it's what we listen to, so this practice helps us to flip the switch and put the chaos in its place.

Change Me Into

When my husband and I walk into the container store I get excited. This store is everything I'm not and would love to be. While Bryan is very organized and everything has its place, which is the reason for the container store visit, I believe my disorganization is the way I organize. I'll know exactly what pile that one piece of paper I need is in, and when someone comes in and cleans my office, I can no longer find anything. I know that just looking at the desktop of my computer stresses Bryan out. The amount of times he's tried to help me create folders is too many to count, and they don't seem to work out for me. So sometimes I'll sit and say to myself, *Change me into the person who is organized*, and suddenly I'm using the folders on the desktop, organizing my piles of books and papers, and feeling productive and satisfied.

This phrase, "Change me into" I took from the author Tosha Silver. She has a book called *Change Me Prayers* (Silver 2015), and the phrase really resonated with me. I played around with feeling the uncomfortable sensation in my body and saying to myself, *Change me into the person who is calm in this moment, who can breathe in this moment, who can be kind in this moment.*

It's not about changing who you are to become something different; it's simply helping yourself pause in the moment to shift out of the stressful state and invite a new one in.

Think about what you'd like to be like in these difficult and awkward, high-stress conversations you get into. Know what you'd like to feel like within them and what you need for them to go well. Those then become what you ask for at the moment.

- Change me into the person who can listen right now.
- Change me into the person who can take a breath and then speak.
- Change me into the person who doesn't say something mean.
- Change me into the person who . . .

Let It Go

Usually there's urgency within our hard conversations. There's a reason they have to happen now and the issues need to be dealt with or else something will fall apart. While the conversation is hard in and of itself, the pressure we put on these moments is even more difficult because in our minds, these are make-or-break moments—how we act and what we say today is it. Impermanence is an interesting concept because there's two sides to it. On one hand it can be used as a motivator to have these conversations and when used in this way, it can keep us in a state of panic, and on the other hand it can be used to help slow down the conversations we're having and help us feel more open and relaxed.

It's hard to remember when we're in a conversation that this isn't the only conversation that we have to have about the topic, that we can stop a conversation and come back to it when we're feeling more clarity and regulated. This reminder within a heated conversation can help us soften and allow more space to do what's best for the conversation itself. *This is only a conversation just like any other; there can be another conversation; I can have a second chance at this. Let it go. Let it go. Let it go.*

What's Helpful to Do

What I've found helpful is to mix the need to say phrases with some of the "own your discomfort" practices. So while you're saying "soften, soften, soften," you're tapping or doing hand circles on your chest, or when you're saying "neutral" or "let it go," you're massaging the webbing between your thumb and index finger. The combination of talk and touch is quite powerful in reducing stress and anxiety.

Think of yourself like one of your favorite athletes in competition. Each time you feel the pressure in a difficult conversation, it's as if you're on the free throw line in front of thousands of people or it's the final minute of the Super Bowl. There's plenty going on to distract you, those you're talking with, the noises in the room, the temperature, people walking by, and especially your heart, which is pounding, and the fear, stress, and worry over getting it wrong, making a mistake, letting others down. Gosh, it's extremely uncomfortable to be in these situations, and yet it's these conversations that are essential for the growth of your team and the company. Next time you're in the playoffs, talk yourself through it, become your own coach, say what you need to say to help you find the pause and continue on.

Make a Commitment

What are three practices that stand out to you? Or what three practices do you think would be the easiest to implement?

Write them down now.

1. _____

2. _____

3. _____

Choose one practice to try.

_____

CHAPTER

9

SOFTEN Meditation Practices

Meditation makes the entire nervous system go into a field of coherence.

—Deepak Chopra

We've covered a lot of ground together so far. And if you're still with me, I'm ecstatic you are because this chapter is a bit different than the previous ones. Up to this point we've been focusing on informal mindfulness practices you can do in the moment of a high-stakes conversation. Now, we're going to be switching gears to a more formal practice of mindfulness. What I mean by formal is that it's a practice we set aside time to do outside of the conversation itself. The formal practice of mindfulness is meditation, and meditation is both an ancient and modern technique that reduces stress and reactivity and helps us pause and take stock of the moment we're in (McLean 2012).

You've likely heard about meditation, maybe dabbled in it, tried it and couldn't stick to it, or possibly you made it work and already have a practice. Well, no matter where you fall on the spectrum, what I'm going to share with you here will give you a different lens through which to look at this practice and do the practice.

Whereas years ago there weren't many scientific studies that showed the benefits of meditation, nowadays there are plenty. And what they show is that meditation changes certain regions within the brain, helping to improve memory and decision-making, and increases our ability to be compassionate and empathetic, and it also shrinks the amygdala, which is the part of the brain associated with fear, stress, and anxiety—the fight, flight, or freeze response.

While most people meditate for general stress reduction, I'm more interested in meditation and its connection with how we communicate: how meditation helps us to pause, lower our hostility and reactivity, and detach from the situation we're in, giving us the ability to choose to speak in a kind, honest, and helpful way. What's known is that as we age, our brain becomes more rigid, meaning it's somewhat stuck in its habitual patterns and pathways. And this reactivity that happens in stressful moments is one of those habitual patterns as it's been around likely since you can remember. What science shows is that meditation helps us let go of habitual behaviors; it creates a more flexible brain (neuroplasticity) that helps us respond differently in these same kinds of situations and interactions. What I've found over the years is that there are certain meditations that when practiced help us pause more easily and naturally in intense situations and also increase our awareness of when we need to grab one of the pause practices mentioned in the previous chapters.

Each pause practice mentioned in the previous chapters has its own meditation, and here I'll share with you what they are.

Why Does Meditation Work?

After my first love passed away I was really trying to figure out how to be okay in the world. I was filled with overwhelming fear and anxiety, having problems sleeping, I kept running moments over and over again in my mind that would keep me in this place of sadness. My body was in a constant state of stress, as the uncertainty of it all was crippling. This was the first time I had ever been knocked off course and saw I was climbing without a harness. I think many of us have felt this free-falling sensation, whether it was a time when we've had our own losses, health scares, injuries, or during COVID. It's impossible to go through something traumatic and our body and mind not be affected by it.

Multiple studies have shown that globally, as a consequence of the pandemic, there has been a rise in cases of general anxiety, psychological distress, sleeplessness, and depression (Hawes et al. 2022, Vindegaard and Benros 2020). You've likely seen within your companies the push and expansion of your well-being programs, incorporating more health and wellness to make sure everyone is taking care of themselves, not only physically but also mentally and emotionally. And this is where meditation enters the mix. Where before, meditation was seen as only a Silicon Valley thing, now it's an essential leadership tool. Why? Because it's a scientifically proven practice that helps us handle stressful situations with more calm and clarity, and there's been an increase over the last handful of years of disruptions that require those in leadership positions all over the world to become more resilient. Even the US Marines have seen that after 8 weeks of meditating for only 15 minutes a day, soldiers were better at handling stress and anxiety (Penman 2012). They could stay calmer and more focused in the heat of battle.

What meditation does, just like the informal practices we've been doing, is create a sense of safety within the body because it moves us from our sympathetic nervous system to our

parasympathetic nervous system. And when we're in our parasympathetic nervous system we can see and think clearly during
stressful situations. The only difference here is that we're doing
this for an extended period of time. As you consistently meditate
for 10–15 minutes a day, you develop certain areas of the brain,
such as those that are responsible for memory, compassion, and
empathy, while parts of the brain associated with fear, stress,
and anxiety begin to shrink. It also affects the wandering mind
and the rumination that can go on during a disagreement, meaning it helps us rein it in so that we're focusing on the things that
are helpful instead of unhelpful. It brings us into the present
moment with the interaction, so we can access a place of clarity
to connect in a way that is more human. And it helps us see our
emotions within a disagreement as separate from us, so we become
more of the observer and witness we want to be in our conversations. As the brain changes, so do we, and so do our interactions.
Soon we're no longer reacting to the hard questions, differ-
ences of opinion, confrontation, or challenges, and instead we're
opening the door, pausing, and sitting down to discuss them.

I know that you're busy and the last thing you'd want to add is
another to-do to your list, and this is one of the biggest obstacles to
meditation for those in leadership roles. In every course, workshop,
training, one-on-one I do, I start with a meditation, and it's hard
even for clients to feel okay taking the time to meditate in our ses-
sions while they know their teams are hard at work in the next room.
What's been great is a lot of companies now bring meditation into
their workplaces weekly, quarterly, and it's a company-wide offering,
which makes it easier to schedule into the day. What I usually say
to clients is that it's okay to feel guilty that you're taking this time
away from what you're doing to sit and to bring that feeling to your
meditation practice. Use the guilt of doing it as the reason to do it.
See, the start of every meditation is to meet ourselves where we are,
and most of the time, we're in an emotional state that makes it really
hard to sit. Think, emotional state . . . time to meditate.

The SOFTEN Meditation Practices

After having kids it took me a while to get back into exercising. And when I did, my whole body screamed quite loudly at me. I brushed it off, as one does, and continued through, thinking it would go away. Months later, I was scouring my son's room for baseballs I could lay down on to relieve tension. I finally made an appointment with my friend and incredible physical therapist Cari over at Release Physical Therapy, and within seconds, she knew exactly which muscle was being affected, from where it began, and what needed to be done. She does something called dry needling, and when she finds the right spot the muscle starts to twitch and release. This is how I would describe the SOFTEN meditation practices; they are prescriptive in nature, in that they go straight to the problem and help to solve it.

The following table is where you'll start. Identifying the areas you may need help in and then doing the accompanying meditation technique that supports it. And as time goes on, and you've increased your meditation time to 10–15 minutes, you're then able to do the SOFTEN meditation, which combines all of these in one. Think of it like a wheatgrass shot for your high-stakes conversations.

Let's learn more about each one.

Challenge	SOFTEN meditation practice
S: Identifying sensation in the body and connecting with the body	Body awareness meditation
O: Being kind and nurturing toward ourselves/ validating how we feel	Self metta/Vipassana meditation
F: Being present within our interactions	Breath awareness meditation
T: Finding the breath in stressful situations	Fear release meditation
E: Seeing others with friendly eyes	Metta meditation/cord cutting
N: Not getting caught in the chaos	Visualization/self-inquiry meditation

Sensation: Body Awareness Meditation

We know that our bodies are in a heightened state during these tough situations, and so practicing bringing the body into a relaxed state more often helps us begin to identify the difference between a stressed state in the body and an unstressed state. Think of the stress like a buzz of energy going throughout the body, and it's so loud that we can't hear anything else except it and the vibration of it. When we can turn that buzzing down, suddenly we're able to feel what's going on again.

In a body awareness meditation the first part is to notice the buzzing in the body, the charge within and see whether we can soften and relax it, starting at the head and moving down to the toes.

We put our attention on the different areas of the body and silently say to them, "Relax, soften," seeing in these moments whether we can let the muscles go and find rest in the body.

Once the body is relaxed we start to observe the body, relaxed, and still, what the sensation of relaxed and still in the body feels like.

When the buzz is less loud within, we start to notice a pleasant sensation within the body, and instead of trying to hold on to it and create more of it, we sit with what's here and see whether we can let go of our attachment to the good feeling. Then we notice neutral in the body—remember, those areas that we don't really think about, like behind the knees or the crease of the elbow. Here we see whether we're bored by this sensation and whether instead we can become more curious about it. Ultimately, we move on to seeing whether there is anything unpleasant in the body or discomfort. We then bring our attention to those areas, and instead of trying to fix it, ignore it, reject it, we turn toward it, hold it in our arms and care and show kindness toward it.

From there we can start to bring to mind a situation that causes anger, frustration, or emotional overload in the body. We start to breathe in the challenges we're facing and feel the body in a state of discomfort. As we're here, we notice what sensation is appearing in the body and where the uneasiness lives in the body. Then we sit with the unpleasantness and breathe with it for a few minutes, seeing whether when we bring our attention toward the sensations we see a change in the texture of them, and then toward the end of our time, we say to ourselves three times, *I can let these thoughts, feelings, and sensations go*. We take a few breaths, coming back into the body, and then slowly open our eyes and move back into activity.

The purpose of this meditation is first to know what your version of relaxed feels like in the body, then the different states within the body (pleasant, neutral, and discomfort), and then we want to practice sitting with the uncomfortable sensation, so we start to see it not as something to fear, as a threat, but as something that's okay to feel, to allow in. At the end, we have to clear the uneasiness we've cultivated within, and so we tell ourselves that we can let these thoughts, feelings, and sensations go.

Quick Note

Sometimes when we start to get quiet with our bodies, we feel more sensation—aches and pains. If you notice a story coming on or thoughts wondering why this feels this way, how did this happen, when did this start, gently, say to yourself, *Thanks for sharing*, and move your attention back toward the focus of the meditation itself.

This meditation helps us live more into the body first, thinking mind second approach, and it keeps us in tune with sensation in the body and what our body is doing and feeling in difficult interactions. It also helps us identify where rest lives in the body so that it's an easier place for us to find in stressful moments. Getting to know the states of our body and experiencing all of them is crucial for pausing in high-stakes conversations.

Own Your Discomfort: Self Metta Meditation, Vipassana Meditation

While the other SOFTEN practices have one meditation that helps us to implement them, the Own Your Discomfort practice has two. These two meditations not only help us have an easier time turning toward ourselves in these difficult moments, but they also play off one another. As offering ourselves metta, or loving kindness, can be hard, what Vipassana does is make the metta practice easier because it helps us see ourselves clearly and allows us to be okay with who we are as we are.

Self-Metta Meditation   When we take on the Own Your Discomfort pause practices they can be hard to do because many of us are used to talking to ourselves in more negative ways. We say things to ourselves throughout the day, and most of the time it's quite critical, judgmental, and something we wouldn't say to anyone else. Jill is a senior executive, and on the outside you wouldn't ever think that she's constantly beating herself up on the inside. She is confident in meetings, knowledgeable with workarounds and problem solving, likable, and is always on time and ready for the day ahead. The challenge for Jill is that while others believe she's got it all together, she thinks she needs to be better and do better all the time. There's this voice inside that pushes her to this ideal of perfection that no one, not even her, can reach. This voice comes into our lives as we developmentally become more conscious, and it comes from our past experiences, others' labels of us, through feelings of scarcity and comparison, and it's become a friend of sorts, meaning, it's actually helped us get to where we are today. It's pushed us to study more, go for more, reach the place we're at within our careers. And then— suddenly—it's not helpful anymore. Usually, this is when I meet people, this voice that has been with them for so long is now making things really hard and uncomfortable, and it's causing more problems rather than making life better.

Having this voice walking around with us all the time makes it harder for us to offer care and support to ourselves during stressful interactions. It's like the *Wayne's World* movie's famous quote: "We're not worthy, we're not worthy." So to combat this and make it easier for us to see ourselves as someone we want to help out in tough situations is metta meditation, specifically a self-metta practice.

Metta is a Pali word that is typically translated as "loving kindness," and this meditation is usually used to extend compassion and goodwill toward others, which we'll get to in a later meditation when we turn toward those we're in a conversation with. However, we can also extend metta toward ourselves, as studies have shown it helps to reduce self-criticism and improve self-regulation (Shahar et al. 2015, Galante et al. 2014, Lutz et al. 2008). The more we practice self-metta, the easier it is for us to be able to calm ourselves in an intense situation. This meditation also helps if let's say we aren't able to pause in a conversation, so instead of beating ourselves up for it and getting in our heads about it afterward, having it affect the next meetings and obligations we have on our agenda, we can be friendly toward ourselves and change our language around it, helping us move through the aftermath faster.

This meditation uses phrases that we first extend toward ourselves and then to others. For self-metta, we are only going to focus on offering these phrases to ourselves. There are many different phrases one can use, and you want to think of what you want for yourself in the moment when someone is questioning your opinion, or sharing their discomfort and unhappiness, or when you have to provide someone with critical feedback. The phrases can start with:

- May I know . . .
- May I be . . .
- May I feel . . .
- May I have . . .
- May I live . . .

Phrases I like for the work we're doing here are:

May I feel safe.

May I accept myself just as I am.

May I know peace.

May I know patience.

May I live with ease.

Feel free to create your own phrases if the above don't resonate with you. Five is a great number, as these will be phrases you'll repeat throughout the meditation. For this meditation you'll start like all others, seated on a cushion with your legs crossed loosely in front of you and your hands resting on your lap, or seated on a chair and your hands resting gently on your thighs.

Invite yourself into the session, by starting to pay attention to the sounds around you. Maybe there are birds, construction, maybe it's quiet. Notice what you hear. Then after a moment, move your focus away from the sounds and place your attention on your heart center. For this meditation, you can place your right hand at the heart if you'd like. Begin to breathe in and out of the heart center, no need to force the breath, let it be natural. After a few breaths begin to recite the phrases you've chosen, *May I feel safe, May I accept myself just as I am, May I know peace,*

May I be patient, May I live with ease. Once done with the phrases you can drop your hand if it's been raised to the heart and then see whether you can visualize yourself in front of you. And as you see yourself, say to yourself, *May you feel safe, may you accept yourself just as you are, may you know peace, may you know patience, may you live with ease.* Then let the image of yourself go, and bring your attention back to your heart center, and again say to yourself, *May I feel safe, may I accept myself just as I am, may I know peace, may I know patience, may I live with ease.* You can then drop the phrases and sit in the stillness. Start to circle the head, roll the shoulders back and down, circle the wrists, and slowly open your eyes, noticing the shapes and colors around you, and move back into activity slowly.

For many this is an uncomfortable meditation to do at first because we don't often sit and take the time to say nice things to ourselves, so if it feels odd to do; embrace the weirdness of it, and I promise that the more you do it, the easier it will get and the more you'll be able to easily access the Own Your Discomfort pause practices the moment you need them.

The other meditation that helps us own our discomfort is Vipassana.

Vipassana Feelings are a major player in how we react to others because certain emotions signal to our body whether we're safe or in danger. And most of the emotions cooked up in stressful situations usually fall into the danger category. What if we could find a way for these emotions to not feel like the bad kid in the classroom that gets sent to the principal's office? We are a binary society and love to label things as good or bad. And lots of our emotions, the ones we feel pretty often (fear, anxiety, emotional overload, stress, anger, sadness, frustration, exhaustion, confusion, lack of understanding—the list goes on) have been packaged and written on in big red letters: "BAD." Look at how many businesses are "good vibes only"—that's a lot of pressure to put on ourselves and the company, as "good vibes only" isn't realistic or natural. The more we play into this idea that there are good ways to feel and bad ways to feel, the more we fall into feeling bad about feeling bad, which causes a whole host of problems and communication challenges within our teams. In Buddhism, every emotion has a light and a dark side to it, which means that anger can be helpful for us, it can be what motivates us toward a goal or what inspires us to do something different, while on the dark side it can turn violent and hurtful. I'm just going to say it here—there are no bad emotions; it's how we choose to act out the emotion that could possibly be "bad." To be able to pause and own our discomfort we have to be able to let whatever emotion we're feeling in the moment we're feeling it be okay for us to feel. When we react aggressively or shut down it's because we're trying to fix, get rid of, or ignore the emotion that's come up. Fighting what's in front of us only makes us suffer more.

This letting our emotions be as they are is what Vipassana is all about, and it's also why it's, in my opinion, one of the most challenging meditations and also the most rewarding on the other side. No longer will you be hijacked by your emotion and controlled by it, because you're choosing to radically allow it.

It took me a really long time to love Vipassana meditation because I wasn't used to letting myself feel all that I was feeling. I would rather shut it all down, pretend it wasn't there, and then have it come out in my passive-aggressive behavior later on. And I fell under the spell of "if you feel negative things, negative things will happen" or "if I think negative thoughts, negative things will happen"—so why would I want to sit with these emotions that were "bad" or "negative"? There's a difference between thinking negatively and having emotions. We can stop or change our thoughts about an emotion, but we can't stop the emotion itself. When I first start working with people, the fear when it comes to Vipassana is that they'll get stuck in the negative and the bad feelings and won't be able to get out. What's pretty incredible though is that the more you sit and allow yourself to feel all the feelings such as anxiety, urgency, need, jealousy, envy, nervousness, desire, obsession, fear, and anger, the more you see how they move and change and soon dissipate and sometimes disappear completely (not forever, but for the moment you're in)—all of what we want to have happen during tough conversations. The emotion is so used to being pushed away that when you start to acknowledge it, it feels seen and heard, which is what our emotions want. Remember the swinging door image from earlier? This is us giving our emotions the opportunity to come in and hang out.

Full disclaimer: this will be an uncomfortable meditation at first, and that's okay. We actually want to feel uneasy here because by sitting with the unpleasant emotions we train ourselves to be able to not only navigate them but also lessen their powerful charge. We're basically retraining our mind and body to handle challenges differently, which is great for our conversations.

Vipassana means to see clearly, to see things as they really are, and studies done within hospitals (Penman 2012) have shown that it helps surgeons and medical workers cope better with stress and challenging situations and that those who do Vipassana react less in adverse situations. Studies have also been done within prisons showing how Vipassana helps improve self-regulation and impulse control (Perelman et al. 2012).

And so the meditation begins as the others do, where you're sitting either on a chair or a cushion with your hands resting loosely on your thighs. Then you'll settle the body with a few long, slow, deep breaths, inhaling, starting at the belly and then bringing the breath up the body to the nostrils and then exhaling back down from the nostrils out the belly. Let your breathing return to its natural rhythm. See whether you can feel any emotion that's in the body as you're sitting; maybe it's urgency from rushing from meeting to meeting or anxiety about an upcoming deadline, you may be feeling excitement at an opportunity, and if nothing is there, then you're going to want to call it forward, silently saying to yourself, *I feel anxious, I feel overwhelmed, I feel consumed, I feel obsessed, I feel fearful, I feel helpless, I feel . . .* As an emotion presents itself, stay with it and let yourself be taken by it, feel your body react to it, and while it does, follow the body's sensations and reactions until they've passed on. If at any time the emotion is too strong, you can open your eyes for a moment and then come back, or you can refocus your attention onto your breath.

Meditation isn't always a walk in the park, and seeing clearly isn't meant to be. What it does though is help us see what's really happening in those high-stakes moments so we can catch the emotion, acknowledge it, and let it go before it consumes us.

Focus on the Present: Breath Awareness

Many managers and CEOs feel pulled in all directions all the time. There's rarely a time where they aren't thinking about work and what needs to be done or how to handle something. From email to text, from meeting to travel, the responsibilities are all encompassing, so much that there is no down time; even when they're sleeping some are waking up to jot things down on a piece of paper just to be able to get themselves back to sleep. Does this sound familiar to you at all? The constant switched-on button impairs strategic thinking and has us being more aggressive and impatient in the moments we want to be calm and understanding. This is one of the reasons many leaders have active hobbies—working out, training for or running marathons, doing martial arts, parasailing, climbing mountains or rock climbing, dancing, cooking. These types of pursuits require them to get out of their heads with all the noise and into the present moment. As Electronic Arts CEO Andy Wilson has said: "I train a lot of Brazilian jiujitsu, and you know, when someone's trying to take your head off, you pretty much can only think about that" (Bunea, Khapova, and Lysova 2018).

Finding the present moment and being in it is hard. It's hard because we're so forward focused, thinking about tomorrow and what's to come, and then we're also very past focused trying to learn from our mistakes. We know that the present is where we get a break, a rest, and when we sit to meditate that is what we give ourselves permission to do. I've mentioned before that meditation can be hard for those in leadership because you're driven, always at the ready for whatever the next moment may bring, and each moment and day brings different challenges to tackle than the next. A great way to get yourself to prioritize this practice is to say to yourself, *This is my time to meditate*, and you do, or block it off on your calendar like you would a meeting. What's great about this meditation is that all you need is to follow your breath, to pay attention to your inhale and the exhale.

Breath awareness practice is one of the most common meditations, and it's what I call a home practice, one that you can do on a regular basis. What this meditation helps us to do is to train the brain to be present, to notice distractions, let them come and go, and then return to the moment we're in. It helps us to refocus again and again on the present, and the portal to presence here is the breath. Doing this in formal meditation helps us in tense conversations note our distractions and what's making it hard for us to listen and lead effectively and redirect us back to the present moment so we can soften, calm our bodies, and continue to discuss what may be challenging for us to say and others to hear or us to hear and others to say. I call this sorting fruit.

It's as if you were just given a big grocery cart filled with fruits and vegetables, and all you're doing is putting them in the bins they belong to without getting distracted by their weight, texture, or smell. There's a moment when you're in a heated conversation, and instead of getting caught within the interaction, you sort through what you're hearing, seeing, feeling, needing. There are bins that you have near you, and you're putting what you hear into different bins so you can continue to do your job well.

Start with your legs crossed loosely in front of you and your hands resting gently on your lap or you can be seated on a chair with your hands resting on your thighs. With your eyes closed, start to notice where you feel the breath most clearly in the body. Maybe it's at the nostrils, the cool air on the inhale and the warm air on the exhale, the chest, or the rising and falling of the belly. Wherever you feel the breath, let this be your focus in the practice. You can follow the breath to the top of the inhale and notice the natural pause at the top, and you can follow the breath all the way to the exhale and notice the natural pause at the bottom. Follow the breath. Sometimes you can say to yourself, *I am breathing in, I am breathing out.* When you notice you're caught up in thoughts or stories, meaning your attention is no longer on the breath, gently bring your attention back, saying to the distraction, *Thanks for sharing; now I'm bringing my attention back to the breath*. It doesn't matter how many times you have to refocus on the breath, as that moment when you notice you're not present and then come back to presence is the training that helps you handle the challenging moments more calmly.

Take a Breath: "Put It Down" Visualization

Margaret was burning out pretty quickly. Her calendar was full of meetings as her team was working on delivering materials for a large commercial launch. She was leading the whole life cycle of the launch, and while that in itself was stressful, she was also completely run down because she was redoing the work of those on her team. The challenge for her was to trust that the team could do the work well and that she didn't have to be involved in absolutely everything. Along with redoing the work, she was having weekly one-on-one calls as well as group calls with the team. Her frenzy and anxiety, as well as lack of confidence in those that worked for her, were coming out in her interactions, and as a result her team was doubting themselves more and making more mistakes because of it. A cycle of dissatisfaction had begun. Margaret wanted to stop feeling so stressed all the time so she could not only personally feel better but also so she could support her team and help them do well. A meditation that helped her to be able to take a breath and pause to foster more connection in the moment was the "put it down" visualization. She had to let go of all that she was holding tightly to and find a way to trust her team to do the work without her getting so involved in the details.

Formally releasing fear that is stored in the body helps us stop living daily in the stress response. And by doing that means we're not as quick to react in tough conversations as we'd normally be. When our bodies feel safe, we trust more easily.

This meditation is a bit different than the others we've done because it's a visualization. All that means is that you'll be imagining in your mind's eye and interacting with what you're seeing. You begin by counting down from 10 to bring your body into a state of relaxation, softening the face, shoulders, back, legs, and toes. Once the body is relaxed, you imagine or you can do it physically, putting your hands out in front of you like an open book. And as you sit I want you to bring to mind all that you're scared of right now, all the fears that are here, what you're upset about, who you're upset with, any doubts, worries, frustrations, what's bothering you, and see them traveling from within to your hands. You can say them aloud or silently to yourself; it's up to you. As you continue to label them, they start to pile up into your hands. And soon they start to take shape within the hands, into something tangible that has weight, and you continue to hold this object that your fears and worries have turned into until you can no longer hold it. From there you choose to chuck it over a fence, bury it under the ground, throw it into the ocean, or put it in the trash, maybe even an incinerator. This visualization doesn't take very long to do, so it's a great one to do before meetings and difficult conversations.

Eyes Toward the Other: Metta Meditation

We talked before about metta meditation, though I focused only on one part of the whole practice, the self-metta part. Here what we're interested in is doing the full meditation because it helps us to be able to see those we're working with as people we respect, care for, and want to be helpful to (Hutcherson, Seppala, and Gross 2008). What the research shows is that areas of the brain, such as the insula, which is the home for empathy and emotional processing, become activated, and that the gray matter increases in the area of the brain associated with emotional regulation (Land 2008; Lutz et al. 2008; Leung et al. 2013; Hutcherson, Seppala, and Gross 2015). This means that by practicing metta meditation we become more resilient and are able to handle our reactions differently within tough conversations. One study from 2012 confirms that practicing loving kindness meditation for only seven weeks can increase love, joy, contentment, pride, hope, interest, amusement, and awe (Fredrickson et al. 2008), all of which help to establish and maintain harmonious relationships.

As you know from before, metta meditation uses phrases that we say over and over. And with the whole practice we offer these phrases first to ourselves, then to someone we care about, then to someone who is neutral to us, then to someone who we are having a hard time with, and then to the world. You can use the same phrases you chose from the self-metta meditation or a different set if you'd like. In the following example I'll use a few different sets of phrases so you can experiment with these as well. *May you feel safe, may you be healthy, may you be free from pain, may you be happy, and may you live with ease.* What you want though is to have go-to phrases that you easily remember and that you can feel when you say them.

You'll start in a seated posture either on a cushion with your legs crossed loosely in front of you and your hands resting on your lap, or you can be seated on a chair with your feet planted firmly on the floor and your hands resting on your thighs. Make sure that you're in a posture that you respect and that feels comfortable for you; tuck the chin slightly so you can feel the stretch in the back of the neck. And know that for this meditation the breathing is natural, and as you go through, you may notice it speed up or slow down; that's okay—there's no need to force or control it. To begin, see whether you can imagine yourself standing in front of you. As you see yourself, silently say, *May you feel safe, may you be healthy, may you be free from pain, may you be happy, and may you live with ease.* You'll recite these phrases to yourself two more times for a total of three.

Then you'll let the image of yourself go, and see someone you love and care for in front of you (this doesn't have to be a person; it can also be an animal), and you say to them, *May you feel safe, may you be healthy, may you be free from pain, may you be happy, and may you live with ease.* After the third time you'll let the image of that person go, and now see in front of you someone who is neutral to you (someone in another department that you see often but don't really know) and recite the same phrases to them, *May you feel safe, may you be healthy, may you be free from pain, may you be happy, and may you live with ease.* After the third time, you'll let this image go and bring to mind someone you've been having a hard time interacting with lately—someone at work who is hard for you to have a calm conversation with or listen to. See them in front of you and say, *May you feel safe, may you be healthy, may you be free from pain, may you be happy, and may you live with ease.* After the third time, let the image of this person go, and now imagine that you're flying over the world or areas where there is suffering, and say, *May the world feel safe, may the world be healthy, may the world be free from pain, may the world be happy, and may the world live with ease.*

After you've recited the phrases three times, you'll bring your attention back to your breath, noticing the inhale and the exhale. Then slowly let go of any phrases, images, and the attention on the breath, and sit in the stillness. Slowly circle the wrists, the head, and when you're ready, blink your eyes open, notice the shapes and colors around you, and slowly move back into activity.

Need to Say: Conversation Visualization

When you were younger what did you dream about? Where did your imagination take you? Maybe you remember playing dress up or setting up a restaurant and selling food, or seeing yourself playing for one of the big sports teams. We all at one point or another have used our imagination to feel "as if" for a moment, and as one of my daughter's favorite characters would say, visualization is just a fancy way of saying imagination. Visualizing is something athletes do for their games, they see the shots, they see the bases, they watch themselves doing the moves and making the play. They do it over and over again, downloading it into their system, for the moment to show itself on the court, field, track, and then there's no nerves and doubt, only execution. And though it's something we usually hear and associate with sports, this technique is extremely helpful for challenging conversations.

You can do this before a difficult meeting or a hard conversation you'll be involved in; you can also do this for your everyday conversations with coworkers or teams, and if you've had an interaction that went south, you can revisit the interaction in your mind and replay it the way you would have liked it to go so that the next time you engage with that person or group, you're less reactive and more responsive. Remember, the brain doesn't know what's real!

While we can visualize the conversations going well (and I recommend doing this), what's more important for the work we're doing here is to visualize the conversation not going well, meaning the other person doesn't agree with us or think well of our opinion or decision, or the way they're talking to us feels derogatory—how do we navigate that interaction with integrity? If we see these situations over again in our minds and watch ourselves break the usual pattern of reacting with a pause practice, we're more likely in the moment to draw on the practices we've already envisioned in these conversations. Here we rehearse knowing what we need to say to ourselves so the language in the moment comes quickly.

You can be seated with your legs crossed loosely in front of you and your hands resting on your thighs or you can be seated on a chair with your feet planted firmly on the ground and your hands resting on your lap. Close your eyes and bring to mind a situation you need to address; this could be with a coworker, member of your team, the board, a client, or family member. Once the situation is in your mind, visualize yourself saying what you need to say to this person or group of people. Where are you? What are you wearing? What is your body language like? What are some of the words you're hearing yourself say? Now see the person or group of people challenge you, question you, see their confusion. See them reacting to you. What do you see yourself doing? Saying? How do you find your way through the situation? And what is the outcome? After a few minutes here, take a deep breath in, and on the exhale let the visualization go.

After visualizing the conversation not going according to plan, you can then come back to closing your eyes and imagine it going swimmingly. Visualize yourself saying what you need to say to this person or group of people. Where are you? What are you wearing? What is your body language like? What are some of the words you're hearing yourself say? Then see it going easily, flowing into the outcome you truly want from this situation. See whether you can sit in the feeling of what you're seeing being true. Feel what it feels like to live in this outcome. After a few minutes here, start to take some deeper breaths, and circle the wrists, circle the head, and blink your eyes open, notice the shapes and colors around you, and come back.

Which Pause Practice Should I Use? Self-Inquiry

There's one more meditation I want to mention, and that's self-inquiry. When we're in a heightened state it's important for us to know what pause practice we need or we'll do to help ourselves start to see clearly, listen openly, and be helpful in the interaction again. Normally, we are disconnected from what we need in a conversation, because we're simply reacting to what other people say or we're going off our own agenda. One of the best ways to start to get to know what we want and need to say in a general conversation as well as what we need in a heated conversation is by practicing self-inquiry.

Self-inquiry is where we get quiet and ask ourselves questions. It's not so much about knowing the answers, making them up, or trying to figure it out and fix it; what's more important is that we're taking the time to sit, ask ourselves the questions, listen, and see what surfaces on its own. Ask yourself questions such as: *How can I keep calm in today's conversations? What do I need to say to myself today? What do I need to remember today? What pause practices will I use today?* Sometimes you may hear something back, maybe images will come after the questions, and it's possible nothing comes to you at all. All of these experiences are okay. We're training ourselves in these moments to slow down and take stock of the situation we're in, giving it the opportunity it deserves to be effective and helpful.

For this meditation we sit, settle into the space, bring attention to our surroundings and our breath, and then we move into the questions themselves. You'll ask one question and then leave a space of about a minute, and then move on to the next question. Here's a list of questions you can use to get started.

How can I keep calm in today's conversations?

What do I need to say to myself today?

What do I need to remember today?

What pause practices will I use today?

How can I show up for my team today?

How can I take care of myself today?

Meditation always seems like a good idea, but then you look at your day, and it's like, *How am I going to fit this in?* You won't unless you want to. What I'm hoping is that you see how helpful the above can be for implementing the pause practices and that you'll play around with some of them and see the benefit in action. Start small, a few minutes a few times a week. Maybe you'll build up from there, maybe you won't; the important part is that it's not a have to do, but a want to do.

Meditation Quick Start

All that's required is for you to find a place where you won't be distracted (that means door closed, computer sound off, phone sound off and in a drawer, hold your office calls), a place to sit, and a timer. I recommend either sitting on a chair, making sure your feet are planted firmly on the ground and your hands resting gently on your thighs, or seated on a pillow or a cushion with your legs crossed loosely in front of you and your hands resting gently on your thighs. Next, choose where to focus or anchor your attention (body, breath, sound, mantra, sensation), and then every time you get distracted, you gently say to yourself, *Oh, thanks for sharing* and then refocus back to your anchor. When you notice your attention has left the building, bring it back, and ta-da . . . that's all it is.

The first three weeks: Start with taking five long, slow, deep breaths in the morning before you step out of bed. Inhale 1, exhale 1, inhale 2, exhale 2. They are painfully slow, though that's what we want! Then you'll choose based on what you need and what you're working on which meditation to start, and only start with 5 minutes twice a week. You'll do this for 3 weeks and then move up to 10 minutes twice a week, and then 3 weeks later, 15 minutes twice a week.

Stay at twice a week and between 10 and 15 minutes until your body tells you if it needs more or less and for how long. Please don't meditate every day, unless that's already your practice, because if you do, you will burn out with it and won't stick to it, which means no benefits whatsoever. Also, guided meditation is the best to start with. Then after some time, you'll be craving your own voice more than someone else's.

CHAPTER

10

The Pause Principle in Action

You don't have to get motivated, you just need to get started.

—Mel Robbins

I used to be a development editor for computer books, and one of the series I worked on was the "in action" series. What I loved about the concept was to show the technology in action, what it looked like in real time. And I think for this work, it's important that you start putting the practices in action as soon as you can. So in this chapter, I'm going to give you a jump start to getting up and running with the practices as well as a 30-day pause principle calendar to help you keep it front of mind each day.

The Pause Practice Jump Start

What better way to kick-start the practices in this book than by doing a 5-day challenge? We all have 5 days to see how we can implement something new into our lives. We do it with food, finances, fitness; why not try it with our communication as well?

The 5-day challenge has a different pause practice and meditation you'll be doing for each day of the week. There is also a quick nightly reflection to see changes and results.

Day 1

Day practice: Today's the day we're going to explore sensation in the body so we can begin to implement the daily soften practices that follow. We'll bring our attention to our physical reactions during our conversations throughout the day, notice what the body is doing, and see whether we can identify what our unpleasant sensation is. Remember, this sensation then becomes our cue to use one of the soften practices covered in the book.

Meditation: Today you'll dip your toe into the meditation pool and do a 5-minute body scan. Pick a time of 6 a.m., 7 a.m., 8 a.m., 12:30 p.m., 1 p.m., or 4 p.m. You'll close your eyes and move your attention to the top of your head, seeing whether you can relax the top of your head, and then you'll move to the face and see whether you can soften the face, go all the way down your body, seeing whether you can let go a little in every area. Once you've gotten to your toes, notice your whole body, relaxed and still. Take a breath and open your eyes.

Night practice: Take a minute before bed to jot down what you noticed today with regard to sensation in the body.

Day 2

Day practice: Today we're going to see whether we can pay attention to the sensation in the body while we're in conversation, and see whether when we feel tightness, nausea, a dry throat, we can say to ourselves, *Soften, soften, soften.* After we've done it, we're going to notice how we feel and how the rest of the interaction goes.

Meditation: Pick a time of 6 a.m., 7 a.m., 8 a.m., 12:30 p.m., 1 p.m., or 4 p.m., and take five long slow deep breaths. Inhale, exhale 1, inhale, exhale 2, inhale, exhale 3, inhale, exhale 4, and inhale, exhale 5.

Night practice: Take a minute before bed to jot down what you noticed today when you said to yourself, *Soften, soften, soften.* What did it feel like for you? How did it change the conversation?

Day 3

Day practice: Today we're going to focus on feeling the unpleasant sensation in the body and inhaling the sensation into a fist and then exhaling and pushing it into our leg.

Meditation: Pick a time of 6 a.m., 7 a.m., 8 a.m., 12:30 p.m., 1 p.m., or 4 p.m., and close your eyes and say to yourself, *May I know love, may I know joy, may I know peace, may I be free from suffering, and may I live with ease.* Repeat this three times slowly. Then see someone with whom you're having a difficult time interacting with and say to them, *May you know love, may you know joy, may you know peace, may you be free from suffering, and may you live with ease.* Repeat this three times slowly. Then let the sayings go, and bring your attention to your breath. Take a few long, slow, deep breaths, and then slowly blink your eyes open and move back into activity.

Night practice: Take a minute before bed to jot down what you noticed today when you pushed the energy into your leg. What did it do for you? Did it help? Also, what was your experience with the metta meditation today?

Day 4

Day practice: When you notice the unpleasant sensation today within a conversation, silently ask yourself, *What are my hands doing? What are my feet doing? What is my belly doing?*

Meditation: Set a timer for 5 minutes. Pick your time of day, 6 a.m., 7 a.m., 8 a.m., 12:30 p.m., 1 p.m., or 4 p.m., and you'll start with your eyes closed and your hand on your belly. Start to pay attention to the breath and bring the breath into the belly. Notice the belly rising and the belly falling. Continue to pay attention to the rising and falling of the belly for 5 minutes. When you notice your attention has drifted, not a problem, say the word thinking, or thank you for sharing, and bring your attention back to the rising and falling of the belly.

Night practice: Take a minute before bed to jot down what you noticed today when you asked yourself what your hands, feet, and belly were doing. Did it help you pause in the conversation? Did it change the way you felt within the interaction?

Day 5

Day practice: When you start to feel the sensation rising in the body today you're going to see whether you can look at the person or group of people you're with and silently say to them, *May you know love, may you know joy, may you know peace, may you be free from suffering, and may you live with ease.*

Meditation: Pick your time of day, 6 a.m., 7 a.m., 8 a.m., 12:30 p.m., 1 p.m., or 4 p.m., and to start you'll close your eyes. You'll take a few breaths to settle the body, and once you've let go of any tightness and tension and feel relaxed, start asking yourself questions you're having a hard time knowing the answers to. If there's something you're not sure about, ask yourself the question, and listen. No need to try and fix the situation or force an answer, only listen.

Night practice: Take a minute before bed to jot down what you noticed today when you turned toward the other person or group of people while in conversation. What changed for you? The conversation? The outcome?

Hopefully with the 5-day challenge you can see how doable this work is and how beneficial it is. I chose only some of the practices mentioned in the book; as you know, there are plenty more you can try out. As for the meditation within the challenge, it really is more a taste of these practices than full formal practice. Though even the mini meditations can be quite powerful and easy to slip in during the day.

30-Day Pause Calendar

What most people like about workout programs or going to a personal trainer is that there's a specific routine and plan to follow. You're not waking up wondering what you're doing that day or wasting time trying to find what you're looking for, and this is what inspired the 30-day pause calendar. Sometimes, we just want to follow a plan to start making what we're doing routine.

You can use the plan given in Figure 10.1 or you can take the pause practices you've already identified within each chapter

that you'd like to commit to, and substitute those into the 30-day
pause plan. Again, what's most important is to play around and
see which practices work best for you.

Pause Plan
30 days

1 Sensation + Rub Behind Your Ears	2 Sensation + Rub Behind Your Ears	3 Sensation + Rub Behind Your Ears	4 Sensation + Rub Behind Your Ears	5 Sensation + Rub Behind Your Ears
6 Sensation + Belly Breathing	7 Sensation + Belly Breathing	8 Sensation + Belly Breathing	9 Sensation + Belly Breathing	10 Sensation + Belly Breathing
11 Sensation + Swerve, Swerve, Swerve	12 Sensation + Swerve, Swerve, Swerve	13 Sensation + Swerve, Swerve, Swerve	14 Sensation + Swerve, Swerve, Swerve	15 Sensation + Swerve, Swerve, Swerve
16 Sensation + Stance of Appreciation	17 Sensation + Stance of Appreciation	18 Sensation + Stance of Appreciation	19 Sensation + Stance of Appreciation	20 Sensation + Stance of Appreciation
21 Sensation + Finger Taps	22 Sensation + Finger Taps	23 Sensation + Finger Taps	24 Sensation + Finger Taps	25 Sensation + Finger Taps
26 Sensation + Soften, Soften, Soften	27 Sensation + Soften, Soften, Soften	28 Sensation + Soften, Soften, Soften	29 Sensation + Soften, Soften, Soften	30 Sensation + Soften, Soften, Soften

FIGURE 10.1 30-day pause plan.

Want to try out the 30-day pause plan? Sign up here:

https://www.intentionalconversations.com/the-pause-plan
You'll get daily email reminders with tips from me to help you
start pausing more within your interactions. And here is a link
for you to download the pause principle workbook, which you
can give to your team, do with your team, or try out by yourself:

https://cynthiakane.com

Final Thoughts

Communication is the key that unlocks any door you'd like to go through in life. And when we start to pay attention to it, our lives begin to change. Companies spend lots of money on training and helping their managers communicate. And what I hear from clients is that they're dry, mandatory, and don't stick. I don't see communication as this formal, boring thing—where it fits into this nice box with categories to learn. It truly is this fluid concept where each person has their own way of expressing themselves, with their own language and nuance. Everyone is coming from a different background, with different experiences, education, socioeconomic status—and what we all have in common is our default reactions. We've all at some point been dismissive, passive-aggressive, and lashed out. As Dale Carnegie wrote in *How to Win Friends and Influence People*, "When dealing with people, let us remember we are not dealing with creatures of logic. We are dealing with creatures of emotion, creatures bristling with prejudices and motivated by pride and vanity." These emotions come on so quickly within a conversation that we don't even know they're there, and it's the state of our body that dictates our language and our behavior. So if we want to master these heightened moments, we have to work with what's happening within us in these moments—we have to turn our attention to where I believe all communication begins, and that is in the body.

We soften the body in the moments we want to be hard, and clarity on the next right action is there for the taking.

When I teach this work, I too have to soften, as I'm never sure how leaders are going to respond. Some might pass it off as too woo woo and others may find it too foreign of an idea to implement, and that's okay; it's not going to sit well for everyone. Though, sometimes I dream. And in that dream there's a softening that happens in businesses all around the globe. And I see a map of the world and little blue dots blinking at all hours of the day and night—each dot that lights is someone pausing in a challenging moment and interaction. . . over and over again. Then I take it even further and see the ripple effect, and soon the world begins to move into a more peaceful state—being led with more intention and integrity.

While I've worked with those in leadership roles, I've also worked a lot with employees, and over and over again they're faced with managers who make their lives unbearable. They are overworked, underappreciated, and rarely heard or given a chance to feel heard. What they're trying to do is find ways to pause and handle their reactions in a more professional way or learn how to interact with managers who are reactive, dismissive, or aggressive so they can get further in their career or just have a good day where they aren't stressed. And I want people to know, while, yes, it's important that the employees know how to pause, it's even more important for the managers—as it's their responsibility to model behavior and create a sound environment. My hope is that this work really does reach the management teams within companies because the health of the organization, meaning the well-being of the people within it, we know begins at the top. It's not only the responsibility of the employee to learn how to interact with the manager in these difficult moments; it's the responsibility of the manager to know how to work with their teams productively in stressful interactions and inspire others to do the same.

I hope this book was helpful for you. There are a lot of practices within it, so whichever ones have stuck out to you are the ones to start implementing. Remember these are practices, which means this isn't a one-time deal—they're to be done daily in stressful interactions. The more you practice them, the easier they get. While this book is written for business, know that these pause practices work at home with family, friends, partners, and kids as well. So as you begin to see changes in your working relationships due to the pause, you will also see shifts in your personal relationships. And if you need help, feel free to reach out; I'm here: cynthia@intentionalcommunicationinstitute.com.

References

Baars, B. J., and N. M. Gauge. 2010. "Emotion." Science Direct. https://www.sciencedirect.com/topics/medicine-and-dentistry/triune-brain#:~:text=The%20oldest%20layer%20of%20the,brains%20of%20snakes%20and%20lizards.

Bakker, J. 2017. "The Influence of Self-Talk in Ultimatum and Dictator Games: What You Say to Yourself Matters!" Utrecht University Student Theses Repository. July 7, 2017. https://studenttheses.uu.nl/bitstream/handle/20.500.12932/26341/Bakker%2c%20J.pdf?sequence=2&isAllowed=y.

Bargal, S., V. Nalgirkar, A. Patil, and D. Langade. 2022. "Evaluation of the Effect of Left Nostril Breathing on Cardiorespiratory Parameters and Reaction Time in Young Healthy Individuals." *Cureus, 14*(2): e22351. https:doi.org/10.7759/cureus.22351.

Barkley, S. 2024. "Pressure Points for Anxiety." PsychCentral, January 5, 2024. https://psychcentral.com/anxiety/pressure-points-for-anxiety#:~:text=Union%20valley%20pressure%20point&text=You'll%20find%20the%20union,stress.

Bentley, T. G. K., G. D'Andrea-Penna, M. Rakic, N. Arce, M. LaFaille, R. Berman, K. Cooley, and P. Sprimont. 2023. "Breathing Practices for Stress and Anxiety Reduction: Conceptual Framework of Implementation Guidelines Based on a Systematic Review of the Published Literature." *Brain Sciences, 13*(12):1612. https://doi.org/10.3390/brainsci13121612.

Bunea, E. M., S. N. Khapova, and E. Lysova. 2018. "Why CEOs Devote So Much Time to Their Hobbies." *Harvard Business Review*, October 8, 2018. https://hbr.org/2018/10/why-ceos-devote-so-much-time-to-their-hobbies.

Carney D. R., A. J. Cuddy, and A. J. Yap. 2010. "Power Posing: Brief Nonverbal Displays Affect Neuroendocrine Levels and Risk Tolerance." *Psychological Science, 21*(10):1363–1368. https://doi.org/10.1177/0956797610383437. Epub 2010 Sep 20. PMID: 20855902.

Clare, R. n.d. "Breathing is a 24 Hour Activity." Dental Sleep Practice. n.d. https://dentalsleeppractice.com/ce-articles/breathing-24-hour-activity-randy-clare/#:~:text=It%20is%20widely%20reported%20that, 672%2C768%2C000%20breaths%20in%20a%20lifetime.

Cowley, D. S., and P. P. Roy-Byrne. 1987. "Hyperventilation and Panic Disorder." *The American Journal of Medicine*, *83*(5):929–937. https://doi.org/10.1016/0002-9343(87)90654-1.

Cox, J. 2022. "Can Stress Cause Low Oxygen Levels?" PsychCentral. https://psychcentral.com/stress/can-stress-cause-low-oxygen-levels#oxygen-and-stress.

Cuddy, A. J. C., C. A. Wilmuth, and D. R. Carney. "The Benefit of Power Posing Before a High-Stakes Social Evaluation." Harvard Business School Working Paper, No. 13-027. August 31, 2012. https://dash.harvard.edu/bitstream/handle/1/9547823/13-027.pdf.

Dana, D. 2023. *Polyvagal Practices: Anchoring the Self in Safety*. New York: W. W. Norton & Company, 2023. https://www.amazon.com/dp/1324052279?tag=&linkCode=ogi&th=1&psc=1.

Dana, D. 2024 "The Science of Feeling Safe Enough to Fall in Love with Life." Rhythm of Regulation. https://www.rhythmofregulation.com/polyvagal-theory.

Douglass, E. "How to Disagree with Your CEO (without Losing Your Job)." HRD, March 9, 2023. https://www.hcamag.com/ca/specialization/learning-development/how-to-disagree-with-your-ceo-without-losing-your-job/438974.

Family Chiropractic Chatswood. "7 Ways Your Posture Messes with You." February 28, 2018. https://chatswoodchiropractic.com.au/7-ways-your-posture-messes-with-you/#:~:text=When%20you%20slouch%2C%20inevitably%20your,flight%20system%20of%20the%20body.

Farhi, D. 1996. *The Breathing Book: Good Health and Vitality Through Essential Breath Work*. New York: Holt Paperbacks.

First Nations Pedagogy Online. "Talking Circles." https://firstnationspedagogy.ca/circletalks.html.

Fredrickson, B. L., M.A. Cohn, K. A. Coffey, J. Pek, and S. M. Finkel. 2008. "Open Hearts Build Lives: Positive Emotions, Induced through Loving-Kindness Meditation, Build Consequential Personal Resources." *Journal of Personality and Social Psychology*, *95*(5):1045–1062. https://doi.org/10.1037/a0013262. PMID: 18954193; PMCID: PMC3156028.

Fritsch, J., D. Jekauc, P. Elsborg, A. T. Latinjak, M. Reichert, and A. Hatzigeorgiadis. 2022. "Self-Talk and Emotions in Tennis Players

During Competitive Matches." *Journal of Applied Sport Psychology*, *34*(3): 518–538. https://doi.org/10.1080/10413200.2020.1821406.

Galante, J., I. Galante, M-J. Bekkers, and J. Gallacher. 2014. "Effect of Kindness-Based Meditation on Health and Well-Being: A Systematic Review and Meta-Analysis." *Journal of Consulting and Clinical Psychology*, *82*(6):1101–1114. https://doi.org.10.1037/a0037249.

Hawes, M. T., A. K. Szenczy, D. N. Klein, G. Hajcak, and B. D. Nelson. 2022 "Increases in Depression and Anxiety Symptoms in Adolescents and Young Adults During the COVID-19 Pandemic." *Psychological Medicine*, *52*(14):3222–3230. https://doi.org/10.1017/S0033291720005358.

Hopper, S. I., S. L. Murray, L. R. Ferrara, and J. K. Singleton. 2019. "Effective ness of Diaphragmatic Breathing for Reducing Physiological and Psycho logical Stress in Adults: A Quantitative Systematic Review." *JBI Database of Systematic Reviews and Implementation Reports*, *17*(9):1855–1876. https://doi.org/10.11124/JBISRIR-2017-003848.

Hutcherson, C.A., E.M. Seppala, and J.J. Gross. "Loving-Kindness Meditation Increases Social Connectedness." *Emotion*, *8*(5):720–724. 2008. https://doi.org/10.1037/a0013237.

Hutcherson, C.A., E.M. Seppala, and J.J. Gross. 2015. "The Neural Correlates of Social Connection." *Cognitive, Affective and Behavioral Neuroscience*, *15*(1):1–14. https://doi.org/10.3758/s13415-014-0304-9. PMID: 24984693.

Khorrami, N. 2020. "Gratitude and Its Impact on the Brain and Body." *Psychology Today*. September 4, 2020. https://www.psychologytoday.com/us/blog/comfort-gratitude/202009/gratitude-and-its-impact-the-brain-and-body.

Kross, E., E. Bruehlman-Senecal, J. Park, et al. 2014. "Self-Talk as a Regulatory Mechanism: How You Do It Matters." *Journal of Personality and Social Psychology*, *106*(2):304–324. https://selfcontrol.psych.lsa.umich.edu/wp-content/uploads/2014/01/KrossJ_Pers_Soc_Psychol2014Self-talk_as_a_regulatory_mechanism_How_you_do_it_matters.pdf.

Land, B. 2008. "Study Shows Compassion Meditation Changes the Brain." *University of Wisconsin-Madison News*, March 25, 2008. https://news.wisc.edu/study-shows-compassion-meditation-changes-the-brain.

Leung, M. K., C. C. Chan, J. Yin, C. F. Lee, K. F. So, and T. M. Lee. 2013. "Increased Gray Matter Volume in the Right Angular and Posterior Parahippocampal Gyri in Loving-Kindness Meditators." *Social Cognitive and Affective Neuroscience*, *8*(1):34–39. https://doi.org/10.1093/scan/nss076. Epub 2012 Jul 18. PMID: 22814662; PMCID: PMC3541494.

Loncar, T. 2021. "A Decade of Power Posing: Where Do We Stand?" *The British Psychological Society*, June 8, 2021. www.bps.org.uk/psychologist/decade-power-posing-where-do-we-stand.

Lutz, A., J. Brefczynski-Lewis, T. Johnstone, and R. J. Davidson. 2008. "Regulation of the Neural Circuitry of Emotion by Compassion Meditation: Effects of Meditative Expertise." *PLoS One*, 3(3):e1897. https://doi.org/10.1371/journal.pone.0001897. PMID: 18365029; PMCID: PMC2267490.

Maxfield, D., and J. Hale."When Managers Break Down Under Pressure, So Do Their Teams." *Harvard Business Review*, December 17, 2018. https://hbr.org/2018/12/when-managers-break-down-under-pressure-so-do-their-teams.

McLean, S. 2012. *Soul Centered: Transform Your Life in 8 Weeks with Meditation.* Carlsbad: Hay House.

Missimer, A. 2020. "How to Map Your Own Nervous Sytem [sic]: The Polyvagal Theory." The Movement Paradigm. March 22, 2020. https://themovementparadigm.com/how-to-map-your-own-nervous-sytem-the-polyvagal-theory/.

O'Toole, M. S., and J. Michalak. 2024. "Embodied Cognitive Restructuring: The Impact of Posture and Movement on Changing Dysfunctional Attitudes." *Journal of Behavior Therapy and Experimental Psychiatry*, 84:101955 https://www.sciencedirect.com/science/article/pii/S0005791624000144.

Penman, D. 2012. "Meditate Just Like The U.S. Marines." *Psychology Today*, July 3, 2012. https://www.psychologytoday.com/us/blog/mindfulness-in-a-frantic-world/201207/meditate-just-like-the-us-marines.

Perelman, A. M., S. L. Miller, C. B. Clements, A. Rodriguez, K, Allen, and R. Cavanaugh. 2012. "Meditation in a Deep South Prison: A Longitudinal Study of the Effects of Vipassana." *Journal of Offender Rehabilitation*, 51(3):176–198. https://doi.org/10.1080/10509674.2011.632814.

Petranker, J. 2014. "The Present Moment." Tricycle. https://tricycle.org/magazine/present-moment/#:~:text=We%20can%20only%20act%20in,inserts%20it%20into%20daily%20life.

Proges, S. W. 2022. "Polyvagal Theory: A Science of Safety. Frontiers in Integrative Neuroscience." May 9, 2022. https://www.frontiersin.org/articles/10.3389/fnint.2022.871227/full#:~:text=Basically%2C%20the%20theory%20emphasizes%20that,observable%20or%20imagined%20and%20invisible.

Reynolds, S. 2022. "How the Nervous System Perceives Pleasant Touch." *NIH Research Matters*, May 24, 2022. https://www.nih.gov/news-events/nih-research-matters/how-nervous-system-perceives-pleasant-touch.

Rutgers Business School. 2018. "Dan Schulman, PayPal CEO Keynote Address." YouTube Video. https://www.youtube.com/watch?v=iqv18iuz3V0&t=1092s.

Schreiber, K. How Relationships Regulate Our Nervous System. American Addiction Centers. June 9, 2023. https://rehabs.com/pro-talk/how-relationships-regulate-our-nervous-system/.

Shahar, B., O. Szsepsenwol, S. Zilcha-Mano, N. Haim, O. Zamir, S. Levi-Yeshuvi, and N. Levit-Binnun. 2015. "A Wait-List Randomized Controlled Trial of Loving-Kindness Meditation Programme for Self-Criticism." *Clinical Psychology and Psychotherapy*, *22*(4):346–356. https://doi.org/10.1002/cpp.1893. Epub 2014 Mar 16. PMID: 24633992.

Silver, T. 2015. *Change Me Prayers: The Hidden Power of Spiritual Surrender*. New York: Atria Books.

South Loop Chiropractor. n.d. "Why Good Posture is Important for Your Health." https://www.southloopchiropractor.com/why-good-posture-is-important-for-your-health-podcast/#:~:text=Posture%20affects%20the%20nervous%20system,functions%20at%20its%20optimal%20state.

Tavoian, D., and D. H. Craighead. 2023. "Deep Breathing Exercise at Work: Potential Applications and Impact." *Frontiers in Physiology*, *14*:1040091. https://doi.org/10.3389/fphys.2023.1040091.

Taylor, M. 2023. "What Does Fight, Flight, Freeze, Fawn Mean?" WebMD, June 24, 2023. https://www.webmd.com/mental-health/what-does-fight-flight-freeze-fawn-mean.

UMMC (University of Maryland Medical Center). 2003. "A Patient's Guide to Anatomy and Function of the Spine." https://www.umms.org/ummc/health-services/orthopedics/services/spine/patient-guides/anatomy-function#:~:text=It%20gives%20your%20body%20structure,you%20to%20controle%20your%20movements.

Unstuck and On Target. 2020. https://www.unstuckandontarget.com/.

Veenstra, L. 2016. "Embodied mood regulation: the impact of body posture on mood recovery, negative thoughts, and mood-congruent recall." *Cognition and Emotion*, *31*(7):1361–1376. https://www.tandfonline.com/doi/full/10.1080/02699931.2016.1225003.

Vindegaard, N., and M. Eriksen Benros. 2020. "COVID-19 Pandemic and Mental Health Consequences: Systematic Review of the Current Evidence." *Brain, Behavior, and Immunity*, *89* (2020):531–542. https://doi.org/10.1016/j.bbi.2020.05.048.

Yamada, M., L. Q. Uddin, H. Takahashi, et al. 2013. "Superiority Illusion Arises from Resting-State Brain Networks Modulated by Dopamine." *Proceedings of the National Academy of Sciences of the United States of America*, *110*(11):4363–4367. 10.1073/pnas.1221681110.

Zaccaro A., A. Piarulli, M. Laurino, E. Garbella, D. Menicucci, B. Neri, et al. 2018. "How Breath-Control Can Change Your Life: A Systematic Review on Psycho-Physiological Correlates of Slow Breathing." *Frontiers in Human Neuroscience*, *12*:353. https://doi.org/10.3389/fnhum.2018.00353.

Zou, Y., X. Zhao, Y. Y. Hou, T. Liu, Q. Wu, Y. H. Huang, et al. 2017. "Meta-Analysis of Effects of Voluntary Slow Breathing Exercises for Control of Heart Rate and Blood Pressure in Patients with Cardiovascular Diseases." *The American Journal of Cardiology*, *120*(1):148–153. https://doi.org/10.1016/j.amjcard.2017.03.247.

About the Author

Cynthia Kane is the CEO and founder of the Kane Intentional Communication™ Institute, LLC, a communication institute for professionals that provides a holistic approach to effective communication. Cynthia uses her proprietary process called the Kane Intentional Communication™ Practice and the SOFTEN practices to help individuals pause in stressful interactions and then interact in a more kind, honest, and helpful way.

Cynthia isn't like other communication coaches out there. The whole narrative of her life shifted when her first love passed away unexpectedly in 2011. He was 32.

The minute it happened, her life changed forever. She was a blank canvas, empty.

Out of her loss came this need, desire, to feel good, to feel cared for. But no matter how much other people tried to nurture her, they couldn't.

Little by little, she realized that the only person who could take care of her, make her a priority, make her feel good, was herself. She had to undo a lot of what she had been taught, and if she wanted to change the way she lived in the world, she was going to have to change the way she interacted with it. This meant shifting the way she interacted with herself, others, and in turn her environment.

She had to learn how to communicate differently to lead a more empowered life. And she created a practice of communication to do just that.

Now, what she wants to do is give others the same opportunity. She wants to help them learn how to take care of who they are by paying attention to how they speak in their career, relationships, life!

She is the author of *How to Communicate like a Buddhist*, *Talk to Yourself like a Buddhist*, and *How to Meditate like a Buddhist* and was named by Yahoo as the #2 Communication Coach to watch in 2021. She is a best-selling course author with DailyOm, and she and her work has been featured in national and international publications including *Self Magazine*, *Thrive Global*, *Authority Magazine*, *The Washington Post*, *Woman's Day*, *BBC Travel*, *Refinery29*, *Mind Body Green*, *The Chicago Tribune*, *Spirituality and Health Magazine*, and more. She has been a featured mindfulness and meditation expert on *Great Day Washington*, *Good Morning Arizona*, *Good Morning Connecticut*, and *All About Women – WENG RADIO*. Podcasts she's been featured on: *Mindful Communication*, *TheFutur*, *Office Hour*, *The Anxious Achiever*, *High Conflict Divorce*, and many more.

Companies she has worked with include Verve Group, Million Dollar Roundtable (MDRT), The Council on Foreign Relations, KPMG, Young Presidents' Organization, Edlavitch Jewish Community Center, BroadFutures, Zonta International, Yellow Telescope, Habour West Consulting, Bard College, UNC Asheville, Association for Healthcare Administrative Professionals, Limeade.

Companies who have supported their employees working with Cynthia through their employee assistance programs include Greenpeace International, Elekta, Michigan State University, KPMG, National Partnership for Women and Families, Virginia Port Authority, Griner Engineering, Inc.,

LodgeWorks Partners, L.P., Hall Render, Killian Heath & Lyman PC, Franklin Street: Commercial Real Estate & Insurance Brokerage.

Cynthia has a bachelor of arts degree from Bard College and a master of fine arts degree from Sarah Lawrence College. She is a certified breath coach and meditation and mindfulness instructor. She lives in Washington, DC, with her husband and two little kiddos.

Index

Page numbers followed by *f* refer to figures.

ADHD, 63, 75
Adrenaline, 15, 17, 19
Aggression, 97
Amygdala, 17, 120
Anger, 91–92
Annoyance, 91–92
Anxiety, *see* Fear and anxiety
Appreciation, 93–95
Asking yourself questions,
    89–91
Automatic reaction, 5, 5*f*
Autonomic nervous system,
    17, 22
Awareness, 25–26, 71,
    132–134
Awareness meditation,
    124–125

Baars, B. J., 15
Back breathing, 74–75
Bakker, J., 103
Bargal, S., 78
Barkley, S., 53
Beards, 52

Belly, focusing on your,
    60–61, 146
Belly breathing, 73–74, 114
Benros, M. Ericksen, 121
Bentley, T. G. K., 69
Big deals, 112
Blaming, 90
Blood pressure, 19, 69, 70, 78
Body:
    communication and
      the, 14–15
    and opening up, 97–98
    signals from your, 45, 48
Body awareness meditation,
    124–125
Brain, 17, 105–106, 120,
    122, 136, 139
Breath awareness, 132–134
Breath grabbing, 72
Breathing. *See also* Take a Breath
    (SOFTEN practice)
    diaphragmatic, 71
    and focusing on the
      present, 73

Breathing (*continued*)
  and focusing on the present
    moment, 61
  and "put it down"
    visualization, 134–136
  shallow, 96
Breath pattern, 69, 79–81
Bucket, filling the, 98–99
Bunea, E. M., 133

Camaraderie, 87
Carnegie, Dale, 151
Carney, D. R., 65
CEO temper tantrums, 2, 85
Change Me Prayers (Silver), 116
Chartered Management
    Institute (CMI), 3
Chekhov, Anton, 13
Chest, tightness in, 50, 109
Chest breathing, 71–72
Chödrön, Pema, 55
Chopra, Deepak, 119
Clear, staying, 111
Comfort, feeling of, 87
Communication:
  as body-mind practice, 14–15
  importance of, 151
Compassion (compassion
    power), 68, 91–93
Conversations:
  feeling grounded
    within, 60–61
  high-stake, 68
  identifying your sensations
    during, 40
  planning for, 30
Conversation visualization,
    138–140

Co-regulation, 47, 51
Cortisol (stress hormone), 15,
    17, 19, 65
COVID-19 pandemic, 3–4, 24,
    76, 104–105, 121
Cowley and Roy-Byrne
    (1987), 70–71
Cox, J., 69
Craighead, D. H., 73–74
Criticism, dealing with, 46
Cuddy, A. J., 65
Cycle of reactivity, 17, 18*f*, 24
Cycle of softening, 24*f*

Dana, D., 47
Dante Alighieri, 79
Default reaction, 5. *See also*
    Automatic reaction
Defense, state of, 22
Diaphragmatic breathing, 71
Discomfort, 27. *See also* Own
    Your Discomfort
    (SOFTEN practice)
Disengaging, 109–110
The Divine Comedy (Dante), 79
Dogs, 50–51
Dry needling, 123
Dysregulation, 49, 75

Ears:
  pulling down on your, 51
  rubbing behind your, 50–51
Einstein, Albert, 25
Electronic Arts, 133
Emotions:
  neutrality of, 130
  self-talk and, 103
  thoughts about, 130–131

Emotional overload,
112–113
Empathy, 35, 136
Employees, 2–4, 50, 76,
104–105, 107–109,
152
Exhaling, 19, 61, 74–78, 80,
106, 111, 133–134
Eyes, closing your, 41
Eyes toward Another
(SOFTEN practice),
29–30, 83–99
and appreciation, 93–95
and asking yourself
questions, 89–91
and filling someone's
bucket, 98–99
how it works, 85–88
and opening up, 97–98
and power of compassion,
91–93
and relaxing your
eyes, 95–97

Farhi, D., 71
Fear and anxiety, 17, 70,
111, 120, 135
Feel-good hormones, 19
Feet:
breathing into the,
75–76
focusing on your, 60
Fight, flight, freeze response,
15–17, 28, 50,
64, 77, 87
Filling the bucket, 98–99
Finger pointing, 90
Finger push breathing, 77–78

Finger taps, 53
First Nations, 86
5-day pause chal-
lenge, 144–147
Five-part breath pattern,
80–81
Focus on the Present
(SOFTEN practice),
28–29, 55–66
breathing, 61
feet/hands/belly, 60–61
holding things, 63–64
how it works, 57–59
internal broadcasting,
65–66
posture, 64–65
senses, 61–63
thumb-to-pinky taps, 64
Food, 62–63
Forbes, 2
Four-part breath pattern,
80
Frankl, Viktor, 5
Frederickson, B. L., 136
Fritsch, J., 103
Frontline managers, 4
Frozen breathing, 72

Galante, J., 127
Gallup, 4
Gandhi, Mahatma, 22
Gartner, 2–3
Gauge, N. M., 15
Goal-directed self-talk, 103
Godin, Seth, 1
Google, 85
Grimm, Brothers, 102
Gross, J. J., 136

Hand, pressure points on the, 53–54
Hands:
    focusing on your, 60
    holding things in your, 63–64
Havening touch techniques, 52
Hawes, M. T., 121
Heart rate, 19, 70, 94
Hegu pressure point, 53–54
High-stakes conversations, 68
Holding things, 63–64
Ho'oponopono (Hawaiian chant), 53
Hopper, S. I., 70
Hormones, 15, 17, 19
Hospitals, 131
How to Win Friends and Influence People (Carnegie), 151
Hutcherson, C. A., 136
Huxley, Aldous, 77
Hybrid employees, 104–105

Indian astrology, 64
Inhaling, 61, 72, 77–78, 80, 134
Inner Frontier Gate Point, 54
Inner voice, 126–127
Instinct, 86–87
Insula, 136
Internal broadcasting, 65–66
Interoception, 36
Interviewing, 38–40
Irritation, 91–92

Jaw line, massaging your, 52

Kalanick, Travis, 2
Khapova, S. N., 133
Khorrami, N., 87, 95
Kornfield, Jack, 45
Kross, Ethan, 103
Kush balls, 63

Labeling, 129–130
Land, B., 136
Leadership, 2, 4, 23, 35, 121
"The Learning Habits of Leaders and Managers" report, 2
Left nostril breathing, 78–79
Lengthening the exhale, 76–77
Letting things go, 117–118
Leung, M. K., 136
"Lightning bolts" reactions, 27, 28
Loncar, T., 65
Lutz, A. J., 127, 136
Lysova, E., 133

McLean, S., 119
"The Magic Porridge Pot" (Brothers Grimm), 102
Managers, 3, 4, 152–153
Mansfield, Ohio, 114
Manual cars, 113–114
Martial arts, 109
Massage pressure points, 53–54
Massaging your jaw line, 52
McConaughey, Matthew, 65–66
Meditation, 119–142
    benefits of, 120–122

body awareness, 124–125
and breath awareness,
132–134
and conversation
visualization, 138–140
how it works, 121–122
metta, 92, 136–138
and "put it down"
visualization, 134–136
quick start for, 141–142
and self-inquiry, 140–141
self-metta, 126–129
vipassana, 129–132
Meetings:
planning for, 30
using food and utensils
during, 62–63
Meltdowns, 47
Metta meditation, 92,
126–129, 136–138
Me-versus-them mentality, 89
Michalak, J., 65
MillerKnoll, 85
Mindfulness, 6–7, 9, 25–26,
35, 92, 119. *See also*
Meditation
Miscommunication, 3
Missimer, A., 68
Mistrust, 104

Native Americans, 86
Nature, being in, 67–70
Need to Say (SOFTEN
practice), 30, 101–118
and disengaging, 109–110
and going back to
neutral, 113–114
how it works, 103–104

and letting things go, 117–118
and opening, 108–109
and resetting, 110–111
and softening, 106–107
and staying clear, 111
and swerving, 107–108
Nervous system, 15–20, 20*f*,
21, 24, 63, 64
Neuroplasticity, 120
Neutral sensations, 39–40
Nose, exhaling
through the, 80

Open, staying, 108–109
Opening up, 97–98
Orange Theory, 29
Oscars, 65–66
O'Toole, M. S., 65
Owen, Andi, 85
Own Your Discomfort
(SOFTEN practice),
28, 45–54, 126
and emotions, 49
with finger taps, 53
with havening touch
techniques, 52
how it works, 48–49
by massaging pressure
points, 53–54
by massaging the side of
your neck, 52
by massaging your
jaw line, 52
by pulling down on
your ears, 51
by rubbing behind your
ears, 50–51
by touching your
sternum, 51

Panic attacks, 70
Paper, noticing the
    texture of, 63
Parasympathetic nervous
    system, 16, 18–20, 20f,
    22, 50, 64, 70, 122
Pattern, breath, 69, 79–81
Patterns, recognizing,
    105–106
Pauses (pausing), 5–6
    cycle of, 24f
    difficulty of, 13–20
    and softening, 23
Penman, D., 121, 131
Petranker, J., 59
Pinky, 64
Planning, for important
    conversations and
    meetings, 30
Play-Doh, 63
Pleasant sensations, 38–39
Polyvagal theory, 22
Porges, Stephen W., 21, 22,
    87
Posture, 64–65, 97–98
Power of three, 105–106
PowerPlay (camp), 112
Pranayama, 78
Present moment, focusing on
    the, see Focus on the
    Present (SOFTEN
    practice)
Pressure, pausing
    under, 14–20
Pressure points, massage,
    53–54
Prisons, 131

Pulling down on your ears, 51
"Put it down" visualization,
    134–136

Questions, asking yourself,
    89–91, 140–141

Reactivity, 119
Reddit, 83–84
Reich, William, 67
Relaxation response, 70
Relaxing your eyes, 95–97
Release Physical Therapy, 123
Reptilian brain, 15, 17, 28, 58
Resetting, 110–111
Rest, digest, and relax
    response, 18
Rest-and-digest
    response, 16, 50
Reynolds, S., 52
Rilke, Rainer Maria, 79
Robbins, Mel, 143
Rodin, Auguste, 79
Routine, 68, 147
Rubbing:
    behind your ears, 50–51
    of the sternum, 51
Rumination, 122
Rutgers Business School, 109

Safety (feeling safe), 22, 27,
    35, 87, 129
Schreiber, K., 87
Schulman, Dan, 109
Self-inquiry, 140–141
Self-metta meditation, 126–129
Self-soothing, 47
Self-talk, 103–104

Sensation (SOFTEN
      practice), 27–28, 35–44
   in the body, 41–42
   defining, 36–37
   neutral, 39–40
   pleasant, 38–39
   unpleasant, 39
Senses, being aware of
      your, 61–63
Separateness, 84, 88, 97
Seppala, E. M., 136
Shahar, B., 127
Shallow breathing, 96
Sign language, 51
Silicon Valley, 121
Silver, Tosha, 116
SIP (slow down, go inward,
      and get present),
      62–63
Skiing, 114–115
Social behavior, autonomic
      nervous system and, 22
Society for Human Resource
      Management, 2
Softening, 106–107
Softening, act of, 22–23, 25
SOFTEN practices, 25–30.
      See also Meditation;
      individual practices
Somatic nervous system, 16
Sorting fruit, 133–134
Sounds, being aware of,
      61, 63, 128
Spontaneous self-talk, 103
Sternum, touching your, 51
Stomach, 41
Stone Age, 15

Stress (stress response), 15–16,
      78, 92, 119, 120
Stress balls, 63
Stressful breathing patterns,
      71–72
Stupid, feeling, 46
Survival mode, 21, 22, 56, 98
Swerving, 107–108
Sympathetic nervous
      system, 15–20, 20f, 22,
      77, 121–122

Take a Breath (SOFTEN
practice), 29, 67–81
   back breathing, 74–75
   belly breathing, 73–74
   chest breathing, 71–72
   feet, breathing into
      the, 75–76
   finger push
      breathing, 77–78
   frozen breathing, 72
   grabbing, breath, 72
   how it works, 69–71
   left nostril breathing,
      78–79
   lengthening the
      exhale, 76–77
   pattern, breath, 79–81
   and stressful breathing
      patterns, 71–72
Talking Circles, 86
Tanamakoon (summer
      camp), 67–70
Tapping:
   the sternum, 51
   thumb-to-pinky, 64

Taps, finger, 53
Tavoian, D., 73–74
Taylor, M., 15
Temper tantrums, 85
Temporomandibular joint, 52
Tennis, 103
The Thinker (sculpture by
        Rodin), 79
30-day pause calendar,
        147–149, 148*f*
Three, power of, 105–106
Thumb-to-pinky taps, 64
Tightness in chest, 50, 109
Training programs and work-
        shops, 4, 15
Trust, 2, 8, 26, 97, 104,
        107, 108, 135

Uber, 2
University of Maryland
        Medical Center
        (UMMC), 74
University of Michigan, 103
Unpleasant sensational
        reaction (USR), 42–44
Unpleasant sensations, 39
Unstuck and On Target
        (website), 112
US Marines, 121
Utensils, 62–63

Vagus nerve, 50–52,
        64, 70
Van der Kolk, Bessel A., 35
Veenstra, L., 65
Vindegaard, N., 121
Vipassana, 129–132
Voice, inner, 126–127
Voluntary nervous system, 16

Waiting to Exhale (film), 77
Wandering mind, 122
Water, flowing of, 70
Wayne's World (film), 127
Wilmuth, C. A., 65
Wilson, Andy, 133
Winfrey, Oprah, 35
The Wizard of Oz
        (Baum), 106
Words and phrases,
        choosing, 102–104

Yamada, M., 83
Yap, A. J., 65
Yoga, 78

Zaccaro, A., 70
Zen, 23
Ziglar, Zig, 101
Zoom, 105
Zou, Y., 70